"I Can't Believe I'm Buying This Book."

A COMMONSENSE GUIDE TO SUCCESSFUL INTERNET DATING

Evan Marc Katz

TEN SPEED PRESS
Berkeley | Toronto

1🕭

Ten Speed Press
Box 7123
Berkeley, California 94707
www.tenspeed.com

Distributed in Australia by Simon & Schuster Australia,
in Canada by Ten Speed Press Canada, in New Zealand by
Southern Publishers Group, in South Africa by Real Books,
and in the United Kingdom and Europe by Publishers Group
UK.

Cover and text design by Catherine Jacobes
Author photo provided by www.SoulmatePics.com

Library of Congress Cataloging-in-Publication Data

Katz, Evan Marc.
   I can't believe I'm buying this book : a commonsense guide
to successful Internet dating / Evan Marc Katz
        p. cm.
Includes index.
   ISBN 13: 978-1-58008-571-7
   ISBN 10: 1-58008-571-7
   1. Online dating. 2. Dating (social customs)—Computer
network resources. 3. Internet. I. Title.
HQ801.82.K38 2003
306.7'0285'4678—dc22

                        2003022005

Printed in Canada

4 5 6 7 8 9 10 — 08 07 06

"I Can't Believe I'm Buying This Book."

To Mom and Dad,
who taught me the meaning of love
and the value of laughter

Contents

ACKNOWLEDGMENTS

I'd like to thank the Academy. It's an honor just to be nominated and in the company of such—

Oops, wrong speech.

Okay, now I've got it:

Praise be to the Lord Almighty, without whom I wouldn't have the strength to—

Wait, it must be in my other pocket.

Ah, here we go:

Thanks to my agent, Stephanie Lee, who never wavered in her support of this book. She's got a great eye for detail, the patience of a saint, and an online dating profile that will make you pee in your pants. Check her out at Nerve.com under the name—

Damn. I keep getting cut off.

Eternal gratefulness to the fine folks at Ten Speed Press, who were not only wise enough to buy this book but to not change the title either. Aaron Wehner, you are a prophet among mortals, and I hope that your faith in this manuscript and in the medium of online dating justifies itself. Julie Bennett, if it weren't for you, I wouldn't have had to rewrite a single word, so I'm still very angry with you. Seriously, Jules, your uncanny sense of structure and "what works" was immensely helpful, and I hope all the readers appreciate the subheadings, which were entirely your idea.

I'm proud to acknowledge the following friends who were generous enough with their time to read 192 pages of dating advice from me without laughing (to my face): Kerry Asmussen, Howard Bliss, Howard Brodwin, Michael Cann, Mylah de la Rosa, Barron Ebenstein, Lavinia Evans, Toni Gallagher, Daryl Katz, Sara Katz, Tiffany Martin, Stephanie Moore, Steve Motola, and Melanie Pastor. I'm lucky to call you all my friends, even if I completely disagreed with every word of your criticism (which I didn't, by the way).

A shout out to Jennifer Meder and Monica Livingston, who reminded me just how little I know about women with their comprehensive lists of dating no-no's.

Mad props to Lori Gottlieb for understanding the meaning of quid pro quo and for single-handedly hooking up a brother with the finest agency in the Bay Area. Day-em!

My deepest love to my mom. If it weren't for her, I wouldn't be the mama's boy that I am today.

Finally, special thanks to Lavinia, for being my sounding board and alter ego from day one at MatchNet customer service; to Mylah, for being my first (but hopefully not my last) online love; to Barron for being my roommate, my best friend, my writing partner, and my Internet dating confidant; and to Daryl, for overcoming her biases against online dating and being the first person to believe in her big brother's big book.

"I CAN'T BELIEVE I'M BUYING THIS BOOK."

And Why You Should Get Over It, Pronto

I know. You can't believe you're buying this book. It's okay. I can't believe I'm writing it. But, like many things in life, sometimes you choose to do something, and sometimes you find yourself chosen. Let's just say that this book has chosen me as its author.

I've been on seven different online dating services (Match, Matchmaker, JDate, Udate, Lavalife, American Singles, and the Onion Personals), and the first three I joined on two separate occasions. I've corresponded with over two hundred and fifty different women and gone out with over seventy-five of them. Out of those seventy-five, I'd say I've actually dated ten women for approximately a month before the relationship fizzled. Finally, after four years of online dating, I fell in love for the first time with a woman I met on the Internet. The relationship lasted seven wonderful months and opened up a whole new world of caring for me.

My point in calling up these raw numbers isn't to draw attention to my inability to sustain a relationship (although it's been noted, thank you, Mom), or to pat myself on the back for my own studliness (less noted by others, but thanks again), but rather to illustrate what a success and a boon Internet dating has been to my social life.

You see, the Internet's job was merely to introduce me to people, and it served that function well. Over the course of four years, I met women that I never would have met while standing at a bar or sitting in front of the TV. Whether or not a date and I were meant to spend the rest of our lives together is an entirely different book—one that I'm quite sure I'm incapable of writing. Nope, this book isn't about love. It's about online dating, pure and simple. It's about the process of writing an ad, putting up a picture, and letting the chips fall where they may. What I hope you ultimately take from this book is that any-one—*anyone*—can get as much as I have out of Internet dating, just by using a little bit of common sense, patience, and ingenuity.

Who the Hell Am I?

Now, if I were coming at you solely with my dubious dating history, I wouldn't be in any position to write this book. I'm not a noted psychologist, I'm not a telegenic TV talk-show host, and there are undoubtedly a number of people who have dated more than I have. Similarly, most folks can boast more impressive relationship records, and many could tell more interesting horror stories about Internet dates gone awry. If I had a dollar for each of the women whom I've met online who said she was planning on writing a book about online dating, I'd be so rich I wouldn't even have to write this book. Everyone involved in Internet dating has interesting tales to tell—each of which would make for a fabulous *Sex in the City* episode. So to the people who want to read those tales, I say, go watch reruns of *Sex in the City*. This is a how-to book for those who aren't sure that they know how to.

What initially got me to create this Internet dating manifesto was my experience as the leading customer relations consultant for MatchNet, plc. MatchNet, owners of AmericanSingles and JDate among other sites, is one of the largest publicly held online dating companies in the world, and after about two weeks on the job, I realized that I had to pen a book about the subject matter. In talking to approximately forty people a day on the phone, I found that virtually none of them knew how to get the most out of the very services for which they were paying top dollar.

My job at MatchNet, which began essentially as a customer service position—answering billing questions, offering tech help, making sure people's photos got posted—quickly morphed into a sales and consulting gig. Next thing I knew, I became the "date doctor" of MatchNet, the guy that clients were referred to if they wanted to enhance their online dating experience. I can't claim that I assumed that position because I knew any deep truths about the human condition; my qualifications stemmed from having already looked online for women for four years. And, for what it's worth, I also happened to take particular joy in imparting whatever wisdom I had about Internet dating to curious customers.

This wisdom was based not only on personal experience—which is to say, the trial, error, and failures that normally accompany dating prolifically—but also from what I observed by looking at other people's online dating patterns. From my computer at work, I could not only see when a client signed up for our service and how often he or she was using it, but I could also see every single person that he or she wrote to. It doesn't take a genius to observe, for example, that the men who wrote to a hundred women in a month, who didn't bother to put any pictures up, and who wrote five essays with variations on, "I'll tell you later," didn't exactly rake in the responses from the ladies. As I presume they still say in junior high school, "Duh."

My first observation from consulting at MatchNet was that common sense seemed to go out the window when it came to dating—not just on the Internet but everywhere. Writing this book is my attempt to bring that common sense back to the table and give it a prominent seat. It's for this very reason that I started the world's first Internet dating consulting firm, E-Cyrano, which offers essay improvement services and online dating advice. *I Can't Believe I'm Buying This Book* is essentially E-Cyrano for the masses. The reason to buy this as opposed to going to my site and getting a consultation is simple. If you can sit through 192 pages of my first-person ramblings, you can master online dating yourself. Not to mention that I'm much funnier on paper than

I am on the phone, and you will save $85 by buying the book instead. Depending on the generosity of the guy, that can be two dates, one date, or a bottle of wine right there.

Welcome to the New Mainstream

Let's face it. While everybody wants to fall in love, online dating, for better or worse, has been stigmatized for a good long while. Dating websites were once seen as an extension of newspaper personal ads, which were known as an arena for the desperate, lonely, and socially dysfunctional. But at this point, it's undeniable that this medium has become far too mainstream for anyone to dismiss categorically. In fact, online dating is the leading paid content category on the Internet, accounting for 30 percent of all paid content spending. Consumers in the United States spent approximately $215 million on personals/online dating in the first half of 2003, up 76 percent from the first two quarters of 2002 (Online Publishers Association and comScore). Yes, this stuff's even bigger than porn.

So get over it. Everybody's doing it. Attractive people? You bet. Busy doctor/lawyer/executive types? Look around. According to a 2002 poll, higher income college-educated households are leading the online dating trend. You'll be amazed by the quality of the people in the Internet dating world, all of whom are drawn in by the same basic, universal pursuit of love. Everyone's just as curious, open, and vulnerable as you are. They tell me so every single day.

By purchasing this book, you're taking a short-term action for a long-term gain. You'll probably have a few laughs, maybe gain a few insights, and most likely will reverse your dating fortunes the second you're done. So what are you waiting for? Buy it! Quick! While no one's looking!

"WHAT KIND OF PEOPLE DO THIS? YOU, YOUR NEIGHBOR, YOUR MOM, AND EVERYONE STANDING IN LINE AT THE SUPERMARKET."

CHAPTER 1

Accepting That Online Dating Is the Wave of the Present

Ten years ago, no one would have thought that the best and easiest way to meet people would be through a computer. Well, guess what? It is. January 2002: eleven million people visited online dating websites. July 2002: eighteen million people visited online dating websites. December 2002: thirty-five million visited online dating websites. May 2003: forty-five million visited online dating websites (comScore Media Metrix, *New York Times*, June 30, 2003). That's over 40 percent of all the single adults in America. And despite the perception that this is a young person's medium, the top age group in terms of expansion is women, thirty-five to forty-four, followed by men, thirty-five to forty-four. The next biggest group? Men and women, forty-five to fifty-four (Yahoo, Inc., September 2002).

The reasons that Internet dating skews older than Internet gaming are clear. Single thirtysomethings tend to be busier and more financially secure, which means that work is important, but so is love, which is why paying for the service is not an issue. Plus, people in their late thirties are feeling the pressure to get married and have children. The expansion of the middle-aged sector shouldn't come as much of a surprise either. There are over twenty million divorcées out there, and I have to guess that the bar scene is far less appealing when you find yourself partying it up with your kids' friends.

This Is As Good As It Gets?

As ubiquitous as the Internet has become, online dating is still a daring step for generations of people who are accustomed to the more traditional ways of meeting. But the fact that other means of meeting are more established doesn't make them inherently superior. Think about it. Where do people normally meet their mates?

- **Bars?** Yeah, you definitely have a better chance of meeting "the one" if you're drunk. And everyone knows that the highest quality people hang out regularly at bars. (Not to take anything away from the casinos and brothels of our great nation.)

- **Parties?** Like bars except with free booze and onion dip. But unless you're extremely attractive, bold, or smooth, picking someone up in a few hours at a party is not always the easiest thing to do. Being able to ask, "How do you know the host?" gives parties a slight edge over bars.

- **Work?** Fact: breaking up with a coworker will ruin any of the minimal enjoyment you may have previously had on the job. In a poll that I just fabricated in my head, 86 percent of the population would rather be unemployed than work in the same office as an ex. That's some convincing evidence against interoffice dating right there.

- **Church?** You think you need to be smooth in a bar? Try getting someone's digits in the House of God, especially if Mom and Dad are sitting right next to your intended future spouse. Ask yourself: what would Jesus do? I'm guessing he'd hit the Internet as well.

- **Arranged marriage?** A bit antiquated, perhaps, but removing the element of choice definitely makes dating a whole lot easier. Big plus. Let's keep this as a "consider."

- **Blind dates?** I'll pick out my own losers, thank you.

Okay, so what do we have here? Arranged marriage or the Internet? A quick show of hands reveals that the majority of America still trusts their own flawed dating instincts more than their parents' flawed dating instincts. Therefore, arranged marriage is out and Internet dating wins.

Amazing, this democratic process of ours.

All jokes aside, dating online is far easier and cheaper than all of the above options. *Easy* and *cheap* are not two words you want to use to describe yourself, but they're perfect for our online dating purposes. For the same fifty dollars you might blow drinking at a local bar on a Saturday night while approaching absolutely no one, you could have six months of limitless emailing on AmericanSingles.com. Plus, the approach is easier (you don't have to have a suave pick-up line), the rejection is easier (the old drink-in-the-face thing just doesn't work over the computer), and the success rate is higher (because everyone on these sites is single, as opposed to many bar patrons who are just out to have fun with their friends).

However, the main advantage of Internet dating is this: you're getting to know your future spouse/boyfriend/booty call *before* you meet him/her. This is significant and it's worthy of further exploration.

We all know the importance of physical attraction in a relationship. I've had three friends whose serious live-in relationships fell apart due to lack of mutual sexual interest. So I'm not denying that the intangible spark that we all call "chemistry" is an essential component to a budding relationship. I am saying, however, that the way you meet someone can dictate the course of your entire initial conversation, your future interactions, and therefore, the rest of your life.

Text: "Hi, I'm Fred." Subtext: "Can I See You Naked?"

I have this theory about why it's so incredibly difficult to meet people at bars and parties. It works something like this:

It's Saturday night. Boys' night out. Girls' night out. Everyone has a dual purpose—(a) hang out with friends and (b) meet someone of the opposite sex. If you're a guy, most of the time you go home empty-handed. Maybe you talked to someone, maybe not, but probably most of your night was spent talking to your buddies about how hot and inaccessible all the women looked and how incredible it would be if you had the courage to approach a single one of them. If you're a woman, you've probably spent the night fending off the advances of the world's six slimiest guys, who are so immune to rejection that, after one from you, they immediately went five feet down the bar to hit on the next most attractive woman they could find. Yep, it's a meat market out there, yet few people are doing any quality meeting. Here's where my theory kicks in.

Traditionally, it's a man's duty to approach a woman at a bar or party. He can do this in a number of ways. Pick-up lines are usually a good start. One can always try these surefire winners:

> **"I know milk does a body good, but baby, how much have you been drinking?"**

> **"Do you believe in love at first sight, or should I walk by again?"**

> **"Can I have a picture of you, so I can show Santa what I want for Christmas?**

> **"Nice shoes. Wanna have sex?"**

But even if you're as charming and sincere as the above lines would indicate, as a man, you're starting from a tough position. Even if you say something simple and straightforward like, "Hi, I'm Evan," just by approaching a woman, you are making one thing very clear: You want to get in her pants. She knows it. You know it. No matter how you couch it, this fact is what brought you over to her to begin with.

Now if you want to extrapolate things even further, you might even say that the second you approach a woman, she could very well be considering whether you are going to be the father of her children. Don't laugh. It's true. And that's a lot of pressure for a guy. Especially if you believe the fabled factoid that a woman makes up her mind within five seconds if she'd want to sleep with you. In truth, a guy has no say in the matter. But that doesn't stop him from trying. As a result, thousands of uncomfortable conversations take place each day in drinking establishments across America, much to the chagrin of all parties involved, except for the bartenders, who happily drown everyone's sorrows in expensive top-shelf liquor.

Of course, none of this man/woman/sex/marriage subtext can be discussed. Instead we are forced to dance this odd mating dance that has taken place for thousands of years, or at least since the advent of the bar scene. How subtle can you be in making small talk with a total stranger? For most people, the answer is "not very."

Which is why picking up someone at a bar or party is not based on anything more than a first impression. Which is why real world dating sucks and online dating rules. Which is why you're reading this book to begin with. But you knew that.

Contrast the "pick up" with the slower, more personal method of online dating and you too could end up like my friend Teresa (a new Internet dating convert), who recently said to me on the phone: "In the past I would get into a relationship and then get to know the person I was dating. Now I get to know the person before I start dating them." Trite, but true. How often have you met somebody at a bar, gotten a phone number and a kiss, and then started learning about each other during the ensuing first date? How many times have you dived into a relationship because someone was attractive without even considering whether the two of you were compatible? To put it more bluntly, who among us has not had sex with someone without even knowing the color of his eyes? Or whether she has siblings? Or grown children? Or how long he's been out on parole?

Don't be embarrassed. It's called human nature. But just because it's normal to want to jump into the sack with a cute stranger, logic dictates that such behavior doesn't always build the most solid foundation for a long-term relationship. And that's what we're all after, isn't it? Well, isn't it?

Fine, don't answer that.

"PETITE, SHY LATINA WOMAN LOOKING FOR WEALTHY IVY LEAGUE VEGETARIAN SWINGER."

CHAPTER 2

Choosing the Best Site for Your Very Specific Needs

It's not my place to tell you where to sign up first. Suffice it to say, there are literally hundreds of Internet dating websites, and, as much as I'd like to save you the trouble, it's really your job to sift through them to figure out exactly which one (or two, or three) best suits your needs.

The good thing is that no matter what you're looking for, there's probably a site out there for you. A quick Google search reveals countless sites—from the conventional "Single White Male Seeks Single White Female for Long-Term Relationship" type sites to more ethnic/religious focused websites—ones designed exclusively for Christians, Jews, Muslims, Blacks, Latinos, Asians, gays, and so on. There are sites for senior citizens; sites for white women seeking black men; sites for men seeking Russian women (Thai women, Filipina women, Ukrainian women); and yes, Virginia, there are even sites exclusively for people seeking sexual encounters.

Do you not fall into any of those groups? Don't fret, there's more. Much more. There are sites for Ivy Leaguers, for shy people, for vegetarians, for rich people, for exes who are trying to reconcile, for people with herpes, and even for tall people—who apparently are sick of looking down at the rest of us as we scamper around looking for dates.

What I'm saying is that if you can't find a website suitable for your interests, you probably forgot to turn on your computer. So turn it on, start surfing, and get to work.

For the Uninitiated

In case this is the first time you're hearing about online dating, I want to give you a two-paragraph rundown of what to expect. I will then attempt to stretch these two paragraphs for another one hundred and eighty-four pages in order to fill out this book, because it would be a crime to charge $14.95 for a twenty-page pamphlet, don't you think?

Simply put, Internet dating sites are just like job-hunting sites, such as Monster.com, where everyone posts a résumé of his/her credentials. (I love metaphors, so just run with me on this one.) Your "résumé" is known as a profile. Profiles usually consist of a series of photos (optional for you shy types), a basic questionnaire listing your general information (height, weight, occupation), followed by anywhere from two to twenty essay questions. Don't panic or have flashbacks of your freshman-year writing course. The essays here are easy because you already know the answers. They're all about you. The advantage you'll have over other cyberdaters after reading this book is in understanding just how important these essays are. Those who skip them and expect to get results are often sorely disappointed.

Posting a profile on a website is usually free. Browsing to look at other members is usually free as well. The costs of online dating are only incurred when you want to write to someone or, on most websites, when you want to write back to someone who has written to you. An introductory email is the equivalent of a pick-up line, with one tremendous advantage—you are able to craft your letter based on information already provided to you in the profile. Once you make contact, you're on your own. You may email each other for weeks before exchanging phone numbers, or you can meet the very next day for coffee. There are no codified rules, except for the Golden Rule. You'll be thankful if you follow it, because the anonymity of the Internet tends to bring out the worst in people. This is no reason to lose faith in the medium, but rather a truth you have need to accept, just as one must deal with termites in a new house.

Eenie, Meenie, Miney, Moe . . .

Internet dating websites change their look as often as Madonna. When one company comes up with a feature where you can email a friend about a potential match, the rest of 'em are bound to hop on board and do the same. Eventually, all the sites are going to be eerily similar, and why not? If you have the technology to offer the same thing as your competitors, shouldn't you use it? Thankfully, online dating has not become completely homogenized as of yet, which is why this chapter exists.

It would be impossible to go into all of these sites in great detail, but I will provide an overview of some of the top ones with the largest databases and biggest brand names. This is far from a conclusive list, so I would encourage you to do your own research, but these sites are a solid starting point. Before you hop online, however, let's run down some of the things you need to do before investing your time in filling out an Internet dating profile.

Now, I'm not much on making readers do homework, but it may behoove you to get a pen and paper and answer one very straightforward question. Be honest. You might be surprised by what you have to say when you look inside and find out what it is that you're really searching for.

Okay, so what are you really searching for?

Sounds like this would be simple, but it turns out that it's not. And, for reasons that should be readily apparent, you need to figure this one out before you actually go on your first Internet date.

You might be like me—thirty-one and single and craving a serious relationship. Apart from the obvious appeal of going to a sex site designed for people who are looking to get laid with no strings attached, my rational side says that a sex site is probably not the best place to look for my future wife.

But say you're a thirty-five-year-old woman and you've just gotten out of your third consecutive three-year relationship. Intellectually, you know it's probably wise to be single for once, but you may also know that single and celibate is not necessarily for you. Maybe a big site like Match.com might hold some appeal to you. Or a site that has ads specifically for sex with no strings, such as Lavalife. You should not, however, sign up for the Christian marriage website once you angrily slam down the phone on your ex. It's just not fair to the altar boys who are seeking long-term commitments.

Maybe you're a fifty-eight-year-old widow. You had a happy marriage that ended prematurely, but you're still too young and vibrant to give up on men forever. While you're deeply saddened by your loss, you also realize there's a lot of living left to do. The last thing you want to do is take care of an old man in his waning years. No, you're looking for another independent male with whom you can share your free time. A man to take to the theater, a man to travel with, or just a man whom you can bring as a guest to weddings. With this in mind, you're probably best staying off of Adult Friend Finders, which is, to say the least, a bit risqué in its notion of sexuality.

This may all seem obvious, but by narrowing your focus, you make your job of finding the right companion that much easier. It's the difference between saying "I'm looking to move to New York" and saying "I'm looking to move into a one-bedroom doorman building on the Upper East Side, below 86th Street and no more than two blocks from Central Park."

Most people end up on websites based on the recommendations of friends. If you don't have any friends that are Internet dating, please tell them to start. If you don't have any friends who are single, you may want to break up their relationships. If you don't have any friends whatsoever, you should pay extra close attention because you really need a mate. Seriously, knowing which website is most appropriate for you comes down to knowing who you are and what you want, and there's little I can do to help you. That's a job for a psychologist, not an Internet dating consultant.

Diving In—Armed with Only a Modem and Water Wings

What you need to do next is create a new email account for yourself that is dedicated exclusively to your online dating endeavors. Email accounts are often free, or, if not, very cheap, and it'll take you less than a minute to take care of it. Go to Yahoo, Hotmail, MSN, or Earthlink, or call any of your local Internet service providers to get started. The reason that you're setting up a new account is for privacy purposes. For every ninety-eight normal people out there who may write to you, there are two nut jobs. This email account is to prevent those nut jobs from knowing your real name. So if your real email address is, say, benaffleck@aol.com, you don't want to make your new one benaffleck@hotmail.com. Come up with something, anything that you can write down and remember. Most websites have their own mailboxes and hide your email address when you correspond, but some reveal it. Either way, you only have to give out your real name and email address whenever you're good and ready.

Don't Be Like a Guy—Stop and Ask for Directions

Once your email is set up, browse the most popular websites for free to see not only what kind of people frequent the site, and whether there are any in your area, but what user functions the site has as well. Ideally, you will find a website that meets all of your needs, but, like a relationship, some compromise is usually required. For example, although it does have voice technology, an increasingly popular function that most sites will one day employ, Yahoo isn't the most impressive personals site. Its graphic design is nothing special, and its search criteria are pretty standard. But everyone's heard of Yahoo, which is why most Internet daters at some point will probably go there to poke around—regardless of the fancy functions that the site currently fails to offer.

The same name brand recognition applies to smaller niche sites. JDate, for example, is the crown jewel in the MatchNet empire because it's the first and biggest name for Jewish singles in the world. There is no shortage of alternative Jewish dating sites, but they're all playing catch-up to JDate. By being the first Jewish singles site on the block, JDate has developed the reputation of being the place to go. This perception feeds a steady influx of paying customers to a site that is easily one of the most expensive ones around.

Years ago, the site that was technologically most impressive was Matchmaker.com. That has since changed as other services have caught up. Still, Matchmaker offers useful features such as email tracking, practical features such as room for fourteen essays and ten pictures, and cutting-edge features like voice greetings. Now it seems that the greatest advantage to Matchmaker is that it breaks up the country into a bunch of niche sites. Go to Matchmaker and see for yourself. Categories for Mormons, nudists, people from the Blue Ridge Mountains, "silver" seniors, and "big and beautiful" people make this less of a melting pot than a bunch of ethnic neighborhoods existing peacefully next to each other. I highly recommend it if you live in an area or belong to a community where there are enough members (you can browse to find out before paying).

Sister sites Dreammates and CupidJunction are pretty good. Both claim membership of over a million people, putting them in the next tier of sites below Match.com and Yahoo!Personals. They have most of the standard functions that the top websites have, including instant messaging, a conversation log to help you keep track of your contacts, and an online mailbox to preserve your privacy. These two sites are each divided into three "communities": Dating, which is described as "a place where you will meet people looking to hang out"; Romance, "where you will meet people seeking serious, long-term relationships"; and Intimate, "where you will meet people seeking intimate encounters." Lavalife has a similar setup, which, albeit blunt and tacky, clearly guides you to the community that is most suitable for you. You can even post your profile in all three categories for no extra cost. Just realize that "intimate" is not merely a synonym for "close."

I initially thought Friendfinder was going to be as good as Match-maker: aesthetically pleasing and easy to navigate, with some advanced features such as voice messaging and private chat rooms. It even had slots for members to post up to five pictures and a long series of interesting essay questions. The problem with the site—a big one—was that you couldn't browse members for free. I got to see a few pro-files in full and if I wanted to see more, I had to pay for a silver or gold membership, or wait until the next day, when I could check out another handful of people. No, thanks. I want to see what I'm buying before I buy it, and restricting my browsing access isn't gonna encour-age me to look around.

I wasn't all that impressed by Udate and Kiss either. Like Dream-mates and CupidJunction, they're nearly identical sites (Udate bought Kiss in 2001), and they each claim a database of ten million single people. I don't know about that, but they are both sizable and reputable websites. And, I'll admit, there are a few cool functions. You can see a demographic breakdown of who's online when you log on (for example, Age 30–45: 1,929 Guys Online, 1,522 Ladies Online). You can keep track of all of your email activity in an Excel-like chart in the section called "Encounters." The profile questionnaire is also very lengthy and detailed. But the essays are totally de-empha-sized, the layout is tough to navigate, and you can't respond to an email unless you pay for the service (although this holds true for most sites, including Match, as detailed in the chart at the end of this chapter).

The truth is, most websites have something unique to offer. For example, AmericanSingles will let you know who has looked at your profile and who has listed you as a favorite. PlanetOut and BlackPlanet don't just provide personals sections but entire media centers for the gay and African-American communities, respectively. eHarmony and eMode each offer a series of personality tests that are meant to help members with the getting-to-know-you process. There are way more than thirty-one flavors out there and until you check out these sites for yourself, it's impossible to know which ones will suit your delicate palate.

Why Settle for the Rest When You Can Go with the Best?

Still, for my money, if you're going to go large, you should sign up for Match, Love@AOL.com, or MSN Personals, all of which are hooked up to the Match system. Match is the biggest brand name out there, and after nine years in business, it boasts more than 850,000 paying subscribers and a database of more than nine million members. Think of it like shopping at the Mall of America in Minnesota. You can get anything you want if you're patient enough to browse the whole mall. Plus, having all of that cash has allowed Match to take the best functions from the other sites and implement them successfully. Six different kinds of searches, up to twenty-five pictures, video profiles, voice profiles, even a function that allows you to flirt by cell phone—Match has it all. The only downside to Match, of course, is that the sheer number of members can be overwhelming and the competition can be fierce. Then again, if you get good at this, there are worse problems you could have than to be overrun by a gaggle of singles who are dying to meet you.

My own favorite site (and the one that introduced me to my last girlfriend) is run by Spring Street Networks, which combines the personals sections from an eclectic group of over forty websites and publications (including Onion.com, Nerve.com, Salon.com, *The Village Voice*, *The Boston Globe*, *The Austin Chronicle*, and *Jane Magazine*). What's unusual about these personals is that their target demographic is distinct—highly educated urban dwellers with a median age of twenty-seven. This doesn't mean that if you don't have a master's degree or if you're over forty you shouldn't be there, but, on the whole, the people who read these publications tend to be young, intelligent, hip, and well-read. The essay topics don't hurt either: "Last great book I read," "Most humbling moment," "Favorite on-screen sex scene," "Best (or worst) lie I've ever told." In offering more than the standard "More about Me" essay that is utilized by most websites, Spring Street makes it that much easier to distinguish yourself from the pack—which is an essential component of online dating. Almost every other site asks for a personal statement that is essentially like those required by most college applications. Such broad and general questions don't lend themselves to creativity.

Alternatives to Conventional Online Dating Sites

Perhaps the best new site around is one known as GreatBoyfriends.com. Created by sisters E. Jean and Cande Carroll, GreatBoyfriends works under the very simple premise that women want their men "pre-owned, pre-approved, and pre-adored." In other words, if you're looking for a mate, who better to describe him than his ex-girlfriend or best female friend? On this site, a man doesn't write his own profile but has the closest ladies in his life pimp him out instead. Not only is he rated in such all-important categories as "Boy Scout," "Male Ego," "Handsome," and "Ring Buying," but the essays by the woman endorsing him actually carry a lot more weight than any statement he might make about himself.

As a result of its original concept, the site has taken off and has spawned a "brother" site called—get this—GreatGirlfriends.com. Cheeky ratings systems for the women on this site include "Gorgeous," "Mother Teresa," "Bitch in the House," and "Material Girl." Yes, the tone is glib, but refreshingly so, and the shorthand answers that the site provides, such as this one for "Bitch in the House"—"She's, uh, high-spirited."—make a point far better than an average person would. For women concerned about safety, men who don't trust their own instincts, and singles who simply want a little fun in their Internet dating, these two websites are a great place to start.

The other site that has gained increasing popularity but falls slightly outside the scope of mainstream online dating is called Friendster. When you get right down to it, Friendster is nothing more than a real-life game of *Six Degrees of Separation*. You put up a profile and invite other friends to join the site as well. In no time at all, you will find yourself connected to thousands of people, through a chain of profiles that you can see. If Annie invited Matt, who invited Nicole, who invited David, who invited Robyn, who invited me, I can see all of their profiles. This is a total word-of-mouth website, which, like Great-Boyfriends, relies on friends' testimonials to "sell" you. You do have an essay for explaining who you are, but the most entertaining feature is reading what a dozen of your friends think about you.

Another unique feature of Friendster is the alternate manner in which you can meet people—through your specific interests. The more detailed information you provide on your profile, the more people—friends, lovers, potential employers—you can find on the site. List your favorite books, movies, TV shows, and music, click on those listings, and the next thing you know, you're in touch with 753 other fans of *The World According to Garp* or 94 of Debbie Gibson.

Happy Hour Nachos Should Be Free, but Your Love Life Shouldn't

Ultimately, the balance between quality membership and user-friendliness is something for each individual to determine on his or her own. But a universal principle of life also applies to online dating: "you get what you pay for." Free sites often have lots of people, but fewer members who take online dating seriously, as indicated by its clientele's unwillingness to pay. On the other hand, sites are sometimes free because they are new and are hoping to build their client bases. Nothing wrong with that, as long as you realize that on these small sites there will be far fewer profiles from which to choose.

Despite the light tone of what you're reading, this book is for people who are serious about mastering the art of online dating. If you want cheap, go to a chat room. If you want to attempt to fall in love, break out the credit card. If you find "the one," it's money well spent. Even if you don't, it's money well spent. You're not only going to get a bunch of good stories out of your online dating experience, but you'll probably make some good friends as well. You can't put a price on that.

Popular Internet Dating Websites

The chart on pages 18–19 describes popular Internet dating websites using the categories defined below.

Number of photos: How many you can display on your profile.

Cost: Generally offered in monthly increments. A few services are based on "credits," which are contact letters that don't expire.

Auto-renewal: Most automatically renew at the end of the initial billing cycle. Check the site to determine renewal rates.

Number of essays: How many opportunities you have to differentiate yourself from everybody else on the site.

Winks or Teases: Also known as Icebreakers, Whispers, or Collect Calls, these allow a nonpaying member to send a pre-written message to a paying member in hopes that he or she will initiate first contact.

Last logged in/changed: Shows the last time a member logged on or made a profile change. Important because you don't want to write to someone who hasn't logged on for a year. Also valuable because sometimes more recent users go to the top of the search lists.

Free response to email: You can receive emails and respond to them without paying a dime.

Chat room: Forty anonymous people in a room. Ready, set, speak simultaneously!

Instant messaging: When another member is online at the same time you are, you can send him or her a private chat window to try to initiate real-time conversation.

Hide profile online: Many websites reveal when you are logged in. This function allows you to log in and remain online without anyone else knowing.

Block user: This function allows you to block someone from writing to you (on that site) ever again.

DATING SITE	NUMBER OF PHOTOS	COST	AUTO-RENEWAL COST	NUMBER OF ESSAYS
AmericanSingles.com	4	$24.95/mo $59.95/3mo $99.95/6mo $199.95/12mo	$24.95/mo $19.99/3mo $17.50/6mo $16.50/12mo	5
BlackPlanet.com	Unlimited	$19.95/mo $39.95/3mo $69.95/6mo $99.95/12mo	$19.95/mo $16.95/3mo $13.95/6mo $9.95/12mo	3, plus you design your own webpage
CupidJunction.com Dreammates.com	3	Monthly renewing: $24.95/mo; Prepaid (nonrenewing): $59.95/3mo $89.95/6mo $129.95/12mo	$24.95/mo	2
Date.com	2	$24.95/mo $49.95/3mo $74.95/6mo $99.95/12mo	Original price renews at end of subscription	1
Friendfinder.com	5	$19.94/mo $39.94/3mo $79.94/12mo for Silver Membership	$17.94/mo $12.94/3mo $9.94/12mo; can stop renewal online	2, plus 20 optional
Friendster.com	5	TBD	TBD	2
GreatBoyfriends.com GreatGirlfriends.com	4	$20.00/mo	Original price renews at end of subscription	8
JDate.com	4	$28.50/mo $79.00/3mo $149/6mo	$28.50/mo $26.50/3mo $24.95/6mo	5
Kiss.com and Udate.com (powered by Match.com)	3	$24.95/mo $49.95/3mo $74.95/6mo	$24.95/mo $18.95/3mo $14.95/6mo	4
Lavalife.com	10	$14.99/60 credits $24.99/115 credits $39.99/ 200 credits	No	1
Love@AOL Match.com MSN Dating and Personals	26	$19.95/mo $44.95/3mo $79.00/12mo	$19.95/mo $14.98/3mo $6.58/12mo	2, plus 7 optional
Matchmaker.com	10	$24.95/mo $49.95/3mo $74.95/6mo 5 free emails	$24.95/mo $16.65/3mo $12.49/6mo	14
PlanetOut.com	4	$4.95/3days $12.95/mo $29.95/3mo $69.95/12mo	$12.95/mo renewal after 3-day offer; others renew at initial rate	2
Spring Street Networks	3	$24.95 for 25 credits $39.95 for 50 credits $69.95 for 100 credits	No	12
Yahoo Personals	5	$19.95/mo $39.95/3mo $89.95/12mo	Original price renews at end of subscription	3

WINKS OR TEASES	LAST LOGGED IN/CHANGED	FREE RESPONSE TO EMAIL	CHAT ROOM	INSTANT MESSAGING	HIDE PROFILE ONLINE	BLOCK USER
Yes	Yes	Yes	Yes	Yes	Yes	Yes
Yes	No	No	Yes	Yes	No	Yes
Yes	Yes	Yes	No	Yes, for 1 credit	No	Yes
Yes	Yes	No	Yes, for paid members only	Private chat	Yes	Yes
Yes	Yes	Yes, but only one per day without paying	Yes	Private chat	Yes	No
No	Yes	Yes	No	No	No	No
No	No	Yes	No	No	No	Yes
Yes	Yes	No	Yes, for paid members only	Yes	Yes	Yes
Yes	Yes	No	No	Yes	No	Yes
Yes	Yes	Yes	No	Yes, 5 credits/20 min; 10 credits/60 min	Yes	Yes
Yes	Yes	No	No	Yes	Yes	Yes
No	Yes	Yes	Yes, for paid members only	Yes	Yes	Yes
No	Yes	No	Yes	Yes	Yes	Yes
Yes	Yes	Yes	Yes	Yes, 2 credits/30 min; 3 credits/60 min	Yes	No
Yes	Yes	Yes	No	Yes	No	Yes

"FUNNY GUY WITH KILLER BODY AND MONEY TO BURN SEEKS WOMAN WHO DOESN'T BELIEVE EVERYTHING SHE READS."

CHAPTER | 3

Headlines Don't Just Sell Newspapers, Y'Know

The headline-style title of this chapter was originally posted by me on Match in 1998. It doesn't convey any actual information, but I hope it shows you indirectly that I have both a brain and a sense of humor. And, based on my circular reasoning, any woman who doesn't get the joke probably isn't going to be the right woman for me.

Headlines are not part of every online dating profile, but for certain websites, the headline is the first thing that members see about you, along with your picture. You get only one first impression, so it's worth putting a little thought into how you project yourself in this section.

Now, what kind of headline is considered "good" is always going to be a matter of taste. Sense of humor definitely isn't universal, but you can't worry about that. I consider this process to be akin to natural selection: if you don't find me funny online, you probably won't find me funny on the phone, on a date, or in the honeymoon suite. But if you're going to be funny at all, this is the place to do it. Yep, all you need is one solid line to capture the attention and the hearts of Internet daters everywhere.

Ah, there's the rub. Coming up with a witty headline can be quite a tall order, but it's a necessary one. You must make that headline memorable, and, if not memorable, at the very least, not crappy.

I don't think the headline has to say anything about you, although it can. You can put "Single White Female Seeks Her Prince Charming," but then again, what woman is not looking for her Prince Charming? Clichés aren't the end of the world, but I think it says something about you if you can avoid them. Think outside the box. Way outside. Like, the box is so far away that you can't even see it from where you're standing.

Your essays are your chance to tell people who you are and what you're looking for. Usernames and headlines should just be fun and eye-catching. That's it. Just like a good headline in a newspaper should make you want to pick it up to read the cover story, your dating profile headline should make me want to see what else is inside. If you've also got a good essay backing you up, laden with personality, humor, and sincerity, you're going to do great.

If You Can't Come Up with Something Smart, Stupid's Not a Bad Way to Go

My friend Donna tends to veer towards silly when writing her headlines. Utterly convinced that the less meaning it has, the more likely someone is to enjoy it, she likes putting down things like song lyrics or movie quotes. The person who catches on to her allusions is going to write back, if only to prove how smart he is for catching her reference. A little reverse psychology, but it seems to work for her.

As an experiment, Donna changed her headline on the Onion Personals every single day for a week. Each day she received multiple responses, and at least one person per day cited her headline in their introductory email. It's not that these men weren't enjoying her essays, but rather, they found her catchy headline to be just the angle they needed to start up a conversation. Donna's particularly partial to cheesy song lyrics.

Quotes from "We Are the World," "Greased Lightnin'," and the "Oompa Loompa Song" will either hook you or lose you. If they hook you, Donna's now got your attention and you're probably already constructing your response to her profile.

In a way, the song/movie quote thing is a cheap way out of getting creative—I mean, taking someone else's good line requires nothing but the ability to memorize pointless information—but I still feel that for its intended goal it's quite effective. Silly headlines get you noticed. And when you're competing, in a way, against ten, fifty, or a hundred other people for attention, you need every ounce of help you can get.

If it's not your personality to be off the wall, and you want to be sincere instead, then at least come up with something interestingly sincere. Anyone can write "Looking for My Soul Mate" or "Sexy Girl Seeks Sexy Guy," both of which are fine, but generic. Too honest can be dangerous too. For example, you wouldn't want to lead off your profile with "Desperate Guy Looking to Get Laid." Although, come to think of it, there is something kind of funny about that. But only if you're being ironic. Which you're probably not. Nah. I wouldn't take the chance.

They're My Headlines and You Can't Have 'Em

Here are some random examples of some catchy headlines that I hope would compel you to read further into someone's profile. Don't plagiarize them, because if you do, so will a bunch of other people, and suddenly your headline won't seem all that original, now will it?

- **Satisfaction Guaranteed or Your Money Back!!**

- **More Fun Than a Bikini Wax**

- **'Scuse Me, While I Kiss This Guy**

- **If Only the Good Die Young, I Think I Might Live Forever**

- **I Left My Wallet in San Francisco**

- **Wonder Twin Powers, Activate!**

- **If a Train Leaves Chicago Going 30 mph, Why Not Just Fly Instead?**

- **I'm a Bad Mamma Jamma**

- Flattery Gets You Everywhere

- You Are Now Entering a No Chauvinist Zone

If you don't like these headlines, that's fine. I don't take it person-ally. Just make sure you don't start your profile with negative, thoughtless, and bland headlines that will make people avoid you like the plague:

- It's Not Me, It's You

- I'm the Mayor of Bitterville

- Only Men with Hair Need Apply

- Have I Mentioned I'm Rich?

- Don't Hate Me Because I'm Beautiful

- Desperately Seeking Sanity

- How Much More Do I Need to Type?

- Only the Lonely Can Play

- Why Be Picky? I'm Not

- Spoil Me Rotten

Will the Real Slim Shady Please Stand Up?

Not all dating sites employ the use of headlines, but every website has its members register under a username or screenname, a pseudonym by which you are known to the strangers on the site. Some people use their real names, which is a bad move for two reasons. One, of course, is safety, although most stalkers can't do much with your real name unless you respond to the initial inquiry. The second reason to go with a username other than your own is because you can. You are hereby given yet another chance to make a strong first impression.

Most people tend to take one of four routes:

1. Due to the fact that coming up with an interesting name requires actual thought, many people stick with their given names (Howard, Lisa, Jim, Nancy, Tayshaun, Wilma, Ezekiel). There's nothing wrong with being up front, but honestly, you can do better than that.

2. Then there are the folks who want a fun and memorable username but squander the opportunity by using some hackneyed nom de plume (Angel, Nicegirl, BigDan, TLC). Or worse, they'll choose a fake name that just sounds like a regular name. As in, "My name is Frank, but on the website, I think I'll call myself Mike." Wow, Frank, that's creative!

3. Of course, there are the good people of the world who feel that, given the anonymity of the Internet and the desire to attract someone, it might be a good idea to come up with some sort of sexy username (VeniceVixen, SexyLexie, 36Cgirl, Jordan69). Unless you're just out to play (not that there's anything wrong with that), there could not be a worse idea. If you're looking for a real relationship of any sort, you will completely undermine your own credibility by putting out the idea that you're some sort of sex god/goddess. I've listened to nice women complain about the awful guys who don't take them seriously and are just out for sex. Then I've checked out their profiles. Headline: "Looking for a Good Time." Username: "HotBlonde." And she's showing four pictures that she took on her webcam wearing only a bra and panties. Men are expecting to sleep with you on the first date, HotBlonde? Go figure.

4. Once in a blue moon, someone will come up with something distinctive. I won't quote those names here because I wouldn't want anyone "borrowing" them for their own purposes. But for the sake of it, off the top of my head, I came up with a few usernames that I thought were original. I was going for ones that were either playful or somewhat descriptive.

IndianaDreamin'	Oxymoron12
DuChampion	Bowling4Men
Nostalgia Queen	99 97/100 Percent Pure
Mr. Wright	SoulSingingSenior
IrishLassie	RiskyBusiness

Why Mrs. Katz Didn't Name Her Son Tom

At this point, I'd like to bring up Newton's Third Law of Internet Dating: for every one person with intelligent, creative, and funny user-names, there are ten people who label themselves with what I would call "losernames." Tell me if you're dying to meet any of these people:

Hal	TripleD
LosersBGone	BitchonWheels
HotExCon	HeartofDarknes
IloveBradPitt	Whatever
HarvardDoc	Doggystyle
UwantMeSoBad	Afghghfh

Yeah, yeah, so some of you may want to meet HarvardDoc or TripleD. I understand. But such names, while descriptive, focus on the wrong assets and can easily come off as bragging. And you don't want to brag. Listen, it's not like a username or a headline will, in and of itself, make or break your entire online dating experience. But why send mixed messages? If you want to be thought of as a nice girl, don't call yourself "DangerousCurvesAhead." If you want to be thought of as a humble guy, you probably shouldn't dub yourself "God, Esquire." As any woman will tell you, the little things count for a lot, so, before you put yourself out there, make sure you've got the little things like usernames and headlines in order.

"I'M TALL, SMART, FUNNY, DOWN-TO-EARTH, HANDSOME, AND HOPELESSLY UNCREATIVE."

CHAPTER 4

Your Essays as Online Résumé, and Why Pimping (Yourself) Ain't Easy

Okay, you've been unemployed for a long time—gosh, now that you look at it, you've been out of work for nearly three years. You've had jobs before, and you very much want to have a job again. But this time around you're not just looking for *a* job, you're looking for *the* job—an actual career—and you will not settle for less. The problem is, after all this time, you're not even sure there is a right job out there for you. All you know is that in your previous work experience, you liked some things and didn't like other things, but never truly found the perfect fit for you. Thankfully, you gained a lot of insight and realized a lot about what you don't want in a job. And now that your unemployment checks have run out and freelancing has gotten old, you're putting yourself back out there in hopes of landing a precious job in a tough market.

As stated earlier, the quest for love is like the quest for a job. And if you've ever hunted for a job, you know how much work goes into it. Research, résumés, cover letters, business suits, follow-up phone calls, and so on. Well, your personal essays are your online dating résumé, and they should be taken just as seriously. This chapter is the longest one in the book for a reason—just as there is nothing more important in job hunting than that one all-important piece of paper, there is nothing more important in your profile than your essays. (A greater number of respondants in a 2003 Match survey claimed that a well-written profile or sense of humor were more important than an attractive photo.)

If two people are applying for the same job, and one person has a résumé chock-full of experience, detailing the many reasons he'd be right for the job, and another person has a résumé that only takes up a quarter of a page and looks like it was written in five minutes, who do you think will get the position? Come on. You won't even get in the door with a half-assed résumé. People online pay anywhere from $100 to $500 to have their résumés rewritten. Same thing for college application essays. That's up to five times as much as E-Cyrano charges for rewriting people's Internet dating profiles for a service that is just as important. "But," asked one interviewer from InternetWeek magazine, "Why would anyone pay for your services when they could do it themselves?"

Why would you ever go to a nice restaurant if you can cook the food yourself? Heck, all the ingredients are in the grocery store, you've got your cookbook right in front of you, and you're pretty sure that this little black knob thingy here turns the gas on. Still, there's something to be said for a professionally cooked meal. The assurance of quality, the freedom of not having to chop vegetables, and the knowledge that despite your best efforts, you may not be able to surpass the chef's special is usually enough to get you to spend $100 on a meal that you know will be over in two hours.

Internet Dating Profiles, Like Diamonds, Are Forever

Nailing your essays is essential. You can write 'em yourself using this book, or get more personal advice through E-Cyrano, but the important thing is that when you're done, you can put your shiny new profile up on an infinite number of sites for free.

Hey, this is a hypercompetitive world. If you're taking your dating life seriously, you have no choice but to pore over those essays with a fine-toothed comb. If falling in love is as important to you as finding a good job, it's only logical that you'd take the time to make your personal statement the best it can be.

The essay-as-résumé concept is my favorite one—the one I hammer home on the phone during consultations—but the rest of the job-hunting metaphor still applies. Your pictures can be considered your connections. They're what get you in the door, or, more literally, what gets someone to read further into your online profile. Your introductory emails are the cover letters that first capture your boss's attention. And so on. But this chapter is about your essays, or résumé, and how to make them shine so that you get called in for a whole bunch of interviews.

Who Bothers to Read Essays Anyway?

For some reason, the myth pervades that "nobody reads the essays." I can't speak for everybody, but when I go to a profile, once I look at a woman's picture, I skip over the questionnaire and go straight to her essays. I think the way people express themselves says far more than any list of interests possibly could. This is not to suggest that interests or looks don't matter. Looks matter more than anything, if only because you're not going to respond to someone to whom you're not attracted. Yes, there are many people who will get online and write something eloquent like "What's happening, Hotstuff?" to every single person who has perfect cheekbones. But is that the response you want? If you're looking for a substantive relationship, you might want to put some substance (and style) into your profile. Writing something unique and specific is like putting out honey to attract bees. With solid essays, you're far more likely to attract someone who has the qualities that you value.

Of Course, You Might Just Be Insane

The other reason to focus your energies on your essay questions is this: while you can't control how you look, you can control how you present yourself. I'm still amazed at how some of my former MatchNet clients failed to see the value in writing a thoughtful, detailed profile that would distinguish them from the masses. Or, as I used to put it bluntly to the occasional male caller, "If she's got five hundred men who wrote to her, why would she choose you, sir?"

This, invariably, would leave them stumped or, for the more combative types, defensive. "She'll choose me because I'm a great guy!" "All these women care about is the picture anyway." "If you write to enough people, someone's gonna write back." Right. If you can't take responsibility for your lack of success in the online dating world, there really isn't that much incentive to talk to a consultant like me, whose sole goal is to help you improve your results. The people who end up blaming the website, or, more often, blaming the stupid, shallow people on the website, are the same people who will end up suing Philip Morris for their lung cancer or McDonald's for their triple bypass surgery. I wish them all the best of luck in their failure. I would encourage them, however, to remember Benjamin Franklin's famous quote: "The definition of insanity is doing the same thing over and over and expecting different results." In other words, if no one has been responding to your profile, it might be a smart tactic to alter your approach.

It's fascinating that some people actually get annoyed at having to write essays for their Internet dating profiles, as if the time taken to express yourself in order to meet your soul mate is wasted time. These folks would love to just click on a few boxes in a questionnaire and immediately start writing to people. What they fail to consider is how many other people are writing to these same exact members.

Let's say a woman posts a profile and gets a hundred letters in her first three days online. How many people is she going to be attracted to? Twenty, maybe? But she can't conceivably date twenty people at once; so how many people do you think she's going to respond to? Three? Five? Eight? And once you've made the cut based on your pictures, what do you think she's basing her next decision on? Not the questionnaires that indicate your preference in music or your taste in food. Rather it's that "More about Me" section where you describe, in detail, why you're such an incredible catch.

No matter how you slice it, there's a lot of competition out there and there's only one way to rise above it—an inimitable profile. You can't separate yourself from the pack if you're writing the same thing as everyone else.

This is where a good essay comes in handy.

So How Do You Write a Good Essay?

There's no formula for how to write an eye-catching essay. Six rules should be considered, however.

1. You're writing for an audience. Don't forget it.

2. It's all in the details. Adjectives mean nothing. Specifics stand out. Use 'em.

3. Have fun! Nobody responds to negativity (nobody you'd want to go out with anyway). If you're depressed, fed up, lonely, frustrated, or just out of a relationship, you may want to wait until you're in a better place before you put yourself out there again.

4. Nobody likes a show-off either. You can state who you are with confidence without putting anyone else down in the process.

5. For Chrissakes, tell the truth. If you don't, you're destroying any future trust you may have tried to build up, and you're giving all the honest online daters a bad name.

6. One word: spell-check. There are no excuses in the computer age.

To elaborate . . .

You're Writing for an Audience

Think for a second. What kind of person would you respond to? Become that person. Read through a bunch of profiles, see which ones you like, and use them as a stylistic paradigm. If you find yourself drawn to specifics, be specific. If you respond to sincerity, then write sincerely. If you like funny, write funny. One thing you should not do is write too short or too long. Writing too short means that your profile is so terse and generic that you will get dismissed without any consideration. Writing too long means that you likely lost your reader at some point on page three of your essay. Try to find the middle ground. Writing long isn't bad. Writing long and boring is: 150 to 250 words per essay should do.

Occasionally, I'll talk with someone who says, "I don't want to read a whole bunch of crap. I just want to start writing to people." Go get 'em, tiger. Let me know how it goes. Back here on Planet Earth, however, I believe that the point of these essays is to show some personality. Be yourself. Be different. I would not recommend that a woman use her original poetry or a that man list the top fifty reasons why he would be a good boyfriend, but in order to separate the wheat from the chaff, you need to be a little creative. Luckily, you don't even have to be that creative to write creatively. Really. That's what this book is for.

It's All in the Details

I find it interesting that a lot of people see writing as different from talking. I don't. I feel that writing is just talking to the page instead of the person. Yet if you read most people's profiles, they write as if this is some sort of formal thing, like a job application. It's not. Your essays should read like a conversation—albeit a conversation in which you're doing all the talking.

Sometimes when people don't know where to begin in their essays, I ask them to just start talking to me, to start thinking out loud. You ever notice how sometimes a friend is going on and on about some problem she's having with a boyfriend, and while she says she has no idea what to do, somehow, while talking to you, she just happens to hit upon the right answer to her own dilemma? These essays work in much the same way. If you talk long enough about who you are and what you're looking for, you might just find yourself saying something interesting and insightful. Like therapy, but much, much cheaper.

So go on. Pretend I'm your friend. Tell me what you're looking for—in your words, using specific examples. Use key words that you've seen in other profiles and apply them to your own essays. And please,

please, please, be honest with yourself. Every lie that you tell in your profile is something you're going to have to answer to later. Height, weight, religion, profession, income, and yes, even marital status—if you lie about it, you'll have to face the music eventually. If you're in touch with yourself—your wants, your strengths, your needs—you're well on your way to an amazing profile.

Avoid a Shopping List of Adjectives

Believe me, you don't have to be the most articulate person around to excel at this. I just want to read about *you*—not see that mental checklist that everyone has, which is nearly identical to everyone else's mental checklist: you're looking for someone who is attractive, smart, funny, kind, honest, warm, successful, and stable? What a coincidence! Me too! And I'm quite sure everyone else here is looking for that person as well. If we all have the same list, how can we tell who's who? Not only that, but just because someone lists an adjective—"funny," for example—it doesn't mean he/she is. As a result, all these words mean nothing. You need to use nouns, ideally, proper nouns (ones with capital letters such as Evan, Bahamas, or U.S. Junior National Waterskiing Team), to bring your essay to life.

Most dating services have questionnaires to take care of all those adjectives. Up front, you generally answer a series of multiple-choice questions about your interests and charms. Witty, stubborn, worldly, intellectual, playful, athletic, romantic. Whatever. Why repeat these adjectives in your essays? It doesn't matter to me if a woman clicked on a list of her favorite foods: Japanese, French, Thai, Continental. Or the kind of music she likes: rock, alternative, jazz, classical, disco. So what? You're clicking on buttons. "My hair is brown." Click. "I'm Christian." Click. "I make over $50,000 a year." Click. That's trivial. Now tell me who you are. Even specific nouns, when written like a long grocery list ("I like baseball, football, basketball, hockey, soccer . . ."), wash right over a reader without impact.

The essays that come to life on the page are the ones where you feel like you're hearing a person's voice. Who they are, what they want, what they're looking for, what their interests are. Everybody has something fascinating to say about herself. Everybody has his own unique upbringing and diverse set of interests. Yet, somehow, 90 percent of the essays out there read nearly identically.

People tend to respond to essays where they feel like someone is talking directly to them. That's why that "voice" is so important. That's why specifics are so important. And sometimes, even when you think you've gotten specific, you haven't even begun to scratch the surface. Here's a favorite work-related anecdote that illustrates this point.

Making Your Specifics More Specific

I was speaking to a very lonely forty-seven-year-old woman who had lost all faith in her ability to attract men. A quick glance at her profile revealed why. She said nothing about herself. I mean *nothing*. After some initial resistance, this woman finally agreed to look a little deeper within, to figure out what it was that made her special. She called me the following day to ask me to look at her revised essays. They were slightly better. If I recall properly, she had a series of sentences that read something like this:

"I like gardening. I like oldies music. I like live theater."

Specific? Yes. Good? No. As my mom told me a long time ago, it's not what you say, but how you say it that matters. I explained that she could get even more specific with her specifics, and if she did, her essay would rise to a whole new level. She still didn't understand, so, extemporaneously, I did something that I rarely did before I started E-Cyrano: I wrote some material based on her basic premise of gardening, oldies, and theater. Here's what I said should take the place of what she wrote:

"Nothing makes me happier than waking up at 6:30 in the morning and looking out at my tulip garden. I'd take the Four Tops over 'N Sync any day of the week. And I get chills when I think about watching M. Butterfly at the Ahmanson Theater." Compare that to gardening, oldies, and live theater, and I trust you can see the difference.

You can apply this to anything that might initially seem specific. "Sports, community service, and travel" may give a reader a glimpse into your interests. Contrast that with "I've been ice-skating since before I could walk; twice a month, I volunteer to cheer up residents at an old-age home; and I just returned from two weeks on a guided backpacking tour of the Amazon Basin." These kinds of specifics not only make you more interesting, but if a reader can find some connection with you in your essays, if what you write sounds like you're talking directly to her, she's more likely to feel that you're what she's looking for. With just a few extra strokes on the keyboard, you've now piqued her interest. If you've written her first, it will at least be enough to get her to write you back so that you can open up a dialogue.

In Case I Failed to Make My Point— A Big, Fun Chart

Below is a chart I made up to illustrate how your specifics can always get more and more specific. These shouldn't ever read like lists, but rather, as the third column illustrates, they should simply sound like one person talking to another.

ZZZZZZZ	HMM . . . INTERESTING . . .	HEY, WHAT'S YOUR NUMBER?
I like music.	I listen to classic rock all the time.	I've seen the Who in concert forty-two times and would probably listen to Roger Daltrey sing the phone book if he did it in Madison Square Garden.
I like animals.	I absolutely love my dog.	My golden retriever, Tobi, can bark in four different languages, which is remarkable since I only taught her three of them.

continued

ZZZZZZZ	HMM . . . INTERESTING . . .	HEY, WHAT'S YOUR NUMBER?
I like movies.	I like science fiction movies.	I hate to admit it, but I waited in line for thirty-eight straight hours to see the last *Star Wars* movie, and I'll probably do the same thing for the next crappy one.
I like to travel.	I've been all over four continents and am looking forward to conquering a fifth when I have the time.	Having conquered the bulls in Pamplona, the sharks of the Great Barrier Reef, and the anacondas of the Amazon, hopefully my next trip will involve a goldfish in a koi pond somewhere in Japan.
I like sports.	I'm a huge football fan.	My dad and I have had Steelers season tickets on the forty-yard line ever since Terry Bradshaw had a full head of hair.
I like reading.	I always have at least two novels going at the same time.	I'm an avid reader and not that I would have chosen it in my book club, but I couldn't believe how much I enjoyed *The Corrections,* by Jonathan Franzen.
I like the outdoors.	I try to go camping at least once a summer.	Every May, I go up to the Appalachians with my three best buddies from college, a tent, a guitar, and two cases of beer. We usually come back with a bag of bottles and one helluva hangover.
I like smart people.	I appreciate those who continue to take classes even when they're out of school.	My friend just finished a semester in a Postimpressionist seminar at Santa Monica Community College and showed me her textbooks. Suddenly I'm an art history convert. Cézanne rocks!

ZZZZZZZ	HMM . . . INTERESTING . . .	HEY, WHAT'S YOUR NUMBER?
I'm romantic.	I love candlelight dinners.	I'm the kind of guy who will surprise you on a random Wednesday with my special chicken Kiev, rosemary potatoes, a bottle of Chardonnay, and, if you're lucky, some Ben & Jerry's Phish Food for dessert.
I'm lots of fun.	I'm always up for an adventure as long as you're along for the ride.	Karaoke? Rock climbing? Strip poker? Road trip to Vegas? Go on, dare me. I'll do it.
I'm sophisticated.	I enjoy a variety of cultural events.	Whether it's Shakespeare in the Park, a Jackson Pollock exhibit, or a limited release French film, I tend to be the first in line and the last to leave.
I'm unconventional.	I tend to see the world a little differently from other people.	I believe the world would be a better place without TV. I believe that a woman ten years older is far more interesting than a woman ten years younger. I believe that Keanu Reeves is an underrated actor. Just kidding. I'm unconventional, not crazy.
I'm funny.	My friends tell me that I crack them up. At least, my good friends do . . .	Guy hears a knock at the door. He opens it up and sees a snail on the ground. Snail says, "You got the time?" The guy looks at the snail, shakes his head, and throws it across the lawn. One year later, the guy hears a knock at the door. Opens it up. Looks down. It's the snail. Snail says, "Hey pal, what the fuck?"
I'm honest.	I believe in sharing everything with my partner.	I'm so honest that I failed lie detector tests in eight different police precincts in three different states. I mean, uh—

Listen, not everybody can be jokey and pull it off. Your essays have to be an extension of your personality. Just remember that last word: personality. The majority of profiles don't have it. Make sure yours does.

Nobody Responds to Negativity

A lot of people pour their hearts and souls into their profiles, God bless them. Problem is, that's not always for the best. Honesty is good. Diarrhea of the mouth is bad. While I'm the first to advocate the idea that more is more when it comes to putting up a detailed profile, that doesn't mean that every idea that pops into your head is something that a reader will respond to. Tell your problems to your mom or your best friend, not to a total stranger.

Believe me, I'm all about honesty—to a point. For example, any guy knows that the question "Does my ass look fat in these jeans?" only has one answer and it's not "Yes." Lies are necessary for us to function in real life. You saw what happened to Jim Carrey in *Liar, Liar* when he had to say the unadulterated truth. Jack Nicholson in *A Few Good Men*. See what I'm aiming at? The truth is, most people can't handle the truth. The truth is often ugly.

Bring Us Your Angry, Your Sad, Your Creepy, Your Bitter

I once read a profile in which a woman talked about her obsession with John Travolta. She mentioned him in her first essay, "More about Me." In her second essay, "More about the Person I'm Looking For," she stated that her ideal man would also like John Travolta. Her third essay, "My Perfect First Date," suggested that perhaps they could have dinner and then catch some movie starring John Travolta. If this were a joke, it would be very funny in an absurd way. But it wasn't. These were the ramblings of a woman who didn't realize that celebrity obsession is not an attractive trait to display in a profile. It's actually kind of creepy.

Mistakes like this are made all the time. One of the essay questions on the MatchNet sites is "What I've Learned from Past Relationships." Most people state things that are innocuous and harmless: communication, honesty, and trust are important, blah, blah, blah. This is, admittedly, a tough essay to write in a unique fashion. Except for those folks who choose to use this paragraph as a confessional forum, with memorable lines such as:

> *"Don't spend six years married to an alcoholic with a violent streak, especially if he hits your kids too."*

> *"I'm getting over my ex of four years and I figured this would be a good way to get started."*

> *"You can't let him cheat on you over and over again because then he'll think it's okay."*

> *"Never date a psycho woman. Or anyone with more than one cat. Although they're generally the same women."*

> *"Women can be evil and mean and spiteful, but they can sometimes be good friends."*

Warms the heart, no?

These aren't bad pieces of relationship advice. They're truthful, at least in the minds of the authors. But they're poison if you're trying to attract a mate. The people who wrote these essays have so much baggage they'd need two porters to check it all on the plane. Everyone's got issues. Why advertise them? I'd recommend freaking out your partner a few months down the line, once you know they're already into you.

Furthermore, nothing good can come from saying anything negative. People gravitate towards the light, so always keep it positive, positive, positive. For instance, don't put down the very medium in which you're meeting each other. "My friends put me up to this. . ." "I don't have any trouble getting a date. . ." "I don't know what I'm doing here . . ." Well, you know what? I'm here. And as far as I'm concerned, if you're here, you're better off finding the silver lining instead of standing under the dark cloud.

"I'm Just Out of a Six-Year Relationship, What's Your Name?"

It's not smart to be dating if you're not in a good place emotionally. Because if you're miserable, then you can't back up the positive, confident picture that you painted of yourself in your profile. And if you can't back up the positive, confident picture that you painted of yourself in your profile, your façade will be blown off on a first date faster than a cheap toupee.

Some people are not well served by online dating at all. Maybe your last boyfriend scarred you emotionally. Maybe your parents' divorce destroyed your self-esteem. Maybe you gained thirty pounds since you stopped smoking. If so, you may want to be careful before getting on the Internet dating superhighway. This medium can take a large emotional toll on someone who is feeling insecure.

My friend Sheri candidly admitted to me that she dated en masse at a time when she was extremely depressed. In hindsight, it was a terrible move. She did it after a breakup (a very common, if unwise decision) to try to keep herself occupied, but it didn't matter. Regardless of how attractive someone may have found her picture or how charming he found her essay, in person she just wasn't the person she claimed to be. When she originally wrote the profile that attracted her previous boyfriend, she was a confident woman. But when she went on her breakup-induced dating spree, that confidence was temporarily lost within her sadness. In the end, she wasn't being honest with herself and therefore wasn't being honest with her dates either.

I wouldn't deem this offense as an equivalent to putting up an intentionally deceptive picture or lying about your career, but in a subtle way, Sheri was guilty of false advertising. No matter how much she may have wanted to, she just wasn't ready to get out there, and fifteen men ended up meeting her at her worst. It should go without saying that no boyfriends emerged for her during that rebound period.

A similar example occurred when a woman wrote to me about how she really enjoyed my profile and wanted to get to know me better. I looked her up. Attractive pictures, bubbly personality, down-to-earth, definitely the kind of person I'd like to get to know. When we talked on the phone, I found out that she had broken up with her boyfriend just two weeks earlier. I jokingly called myself "the rebound guy" to diffuse the awkwardness, but that's just what I was. After a week of talking on the phone and planning a time and place to meet for drinks, she called me right before the date to tell me that she wasn't ready. I wasn't mad at her. I'd been there myself. But if she had looked a little closer in the mirror, she may have realized that dating so soon after her breakup was probably not the wisest move. I later found out that she got back together with her boyfriend.

We all need a little time to breathe and cleanse ourselves before we can successfully move on from a relationship; if we don't take that time, moving on is rarely going to be successful.

A litmus test to determine if you're ready to date online: If you find that writing your essay was a "cathartic process," well, you might want to hold off for a bit. This isn't the time for therapy. This is the time for confident, creative, and positive self-advertising. If you can't tell if what you're saying is too heavy (and many of us can't because we're too close to the subject matter), ask a trusted friend. You should be getting results from your profile, and if you're not, your tell-all attitude may very well be the reason why.

Nobody Likes a Show-off, Either

By the same token, bragging is never an attractive quality. There's a fine line between confident and cocky, and the difference is largely semantic. Many people are uncomfortable talking about themselves for fear of sounding arrogant, but as long as you avoid self-aggrandizing commentary and patronizing jibes at others, you should be just fine.

Most people stick with list-writing anyway: smart, attractive, funny, successful, kind, romantic, fit, and so on. The list-writers never strike me as braggarts so much as people who are either careless or uncreative. If you want to see arrogant, the essay below is an actual example of self-confidence run amok. Once you read it, I don't think I'll need to explain where this charming girl went wrong.

About Me . . . .

I was born into a very successful family in Bethesda. My parents are extremely well-off. Dad is a tenured professor at Johns Hopkins and Mom is a noted psychologist. I am currently in my second year at Harvard Business School. I have brains, beauty, family, taste, and money. I'm looking for a real man. I doubt any of you are on the Internet, but what the hell . . .

My Perfect Match . . . .

I am looking for a highly successful man, and don't have time to deal with all the unemployed losers out there. If you're under 30, take a hike. Over 40, same thing. If you're taller than 5'11", have a full head of hair, and a career on the rise, you might just get my attention. I'm only interested in very successful men, because they're the only ones who know how to handle being with a strong woman. I've been told I'm intimidating, and honestly, I'm glad. It weeds out the weaklings out there (but apparently not enough). I am financially self-sufficient, but I would like for my man to do better than me, so we can live in luxury together. I am not looking for a sugar daddy. I just know what I want.

Perfect First Date . . . .

You tell me. Your answer will probably say a lot about you. Save the crap about moonlit walks on the beach for someone who cares. Tell me what island we're flying to. What hotel we're staying at. What restaurant we're dining in. Cheap guys, you know where you can go. I am a rare diamond and do not want crappy metal surrounding me.

Ideal Relationship . . . .

An ideal relationship is where both partners know what they want and do not pretend to be something they are not. Put me up on a pedestal, and you will get your just rewards. And if you couldn't tell from the rest of what I wrote, honesty and mutual attraction are very important.

Learned from Past Relationships . . . .

I don't need a man to make me happy.

I can't fabricate a profile that is a bigger turnoff than that one, so I won't even begin to try. Simply put: no one likes a stuck-up bitch. Not even the jackass described in the following.

"Let Me Guess: You Drive a Porsche and Have a Small Penis?"

One time, a brusque businessman in his forties called me at MatchNet to purchase a JDate subscription. I told him that I'd be pleased to sign him up, but that he might want to work on his essays first. He was taken aback. The customer service representative is criticizing his essays? Before he could ask to speak to my manager, I explained that I was a membership consultant and a longtime member of the very website to which he was about to subscribe. And rather than take his credit card number and watch him fail miserably, I'd prefer to tell him up front that a little effort on his profile would go a long way in improving his success online.

Now I had his attention.

His essays were not only short but terribly cocky as well. He mentioned that he was a successful business executive who liked to entertain clients at his pool, on his boat, and at the country club, and that he was accustomed to a very expensive lifestyle. In brief, he did everything but say, "I'm rich! I'm rich!" in his essay. Then, in describing the woman he wanted to meet, he focused solely on the physical aspect, as if all a woman had to offer his kingdom was her body. I couldn't help but think that the only woman who would respond to a guy like this would be an utterly shallow gold digger. Perhaps they'd be happy riding off into the trophy marriage sunset together, but I had a hunch that there was more to Mr. Businessman than his desire for someone "young, slim, curvy, and drop-dead gorgeous."

So I asked him, point-blank: "What do you want?"

"Huh?" he replied.

"What do you want? Are you looking to get laid? Are you looking for a girlfriend? Are you looking for a future wife? Tell me, honestly, what do you want?"

It was as if I had magically punctured his condescending Wall Street veneer. His voice got softer as he told me, "I'm looking to get married again. I really want to fall in love."

I told him that if he kept his essay as is, the only women he would attract were women who wanted him for his money.

"Is that your ideal mate?" I asked.

"Of course not," he said.

I told him that I assumed there was a lot more depth to him than his profile would indicate and that he might want to inject some of that substance into his essays. "If I were a rich man," I told him, "I'd be wary about advertising it, for fear that a woman would want me just for my money."

"Yeah," he said, "I never thought of it that way."

When I informed him that focusing on a woman's height, weight, and figure wasn't the brightest approach either, it all started to come together for him. He realized that while there's nothing wrong with desiring a woman of a certain body type, it's probably not smart to put it out there as the number one priority on your checklist, especially if you're looking to forge a real relationship with a woman of substance.

Any woman who doesn't see herself as drop-dead gorgeous won't feel attractive enough to respond to his ad, and any woman with self-respect will probably avoid a guy stupid enough to display his shallowness for the entire world to see. If you want a hottie, write to a hottie. Just don't tell women that if they're not hot, they need not apply. Even the hot ones will be offended.

Lies, Lies, and More Lies

Where to begin? Everyone's biggest complaint about online dating is about all the liars out there; you know, the people who get online when they're married, the people who shave ten years off their age, the people who claim to be lawyers when they're really convicts. If you listen to all the rumors out there, you'd think that everyone who dates online has something to hide. Many do. These are people with low self-esteem who tell untruths because they're not who they want to be. Not rich, not young, not married, not tall, not happy, not thin. I feel bad for them, because until they're comfortable with themselves they're never going to find true love.

How Do You Think You're Gonna Pull This Off?

A guy can't say he's 6'1", meet you at the restaurant, and then be 5'8" without you noticing. A woman can't be a spry and vivacious forty-five-year-old but also have a thirty-year-old son and two grandkids. Liars end up hurting themselves more than anyone else, because when they start off a relationship with a lie, they pretty much end the relationship right there as well. Did the recipient of the lie waste a little time and energy on the loser who isn't secure enough to admit who he really is? Sure. Could she just as easily have wasted time on this loser in real life? Of course. To massacre a Gertrude Stein line: a liar is a liar is a liar. Online liars are real-life liars. With online dating, you're just finding out the truth a little bit later, that's all.

I often find myself telling people who still feel there's a stigma to Internet dating that the people who do it are no better or worse than the people you'd meet at work, at bars, or through friends. They're the same exact people. But because they can hide behind a pseudonym and a computer until that fateful first date, certain low-self-esteem folks are emboldened to make claims about themselves that they can't necessarily back up. And unlike meeting someone at a party, you don't have any character witnesses to double-check the veracity of a prospect's statements.

So proceed cautiously, taking in all of a person's information with detached bemusement and perhaps an extra grain of salt. Don't spend too much time wondering whether the person on the phone is being honest. Assume he is. But if he's not, don't be surprised. While it's appalling to find out how many people lie, the best you can do on your part is to tell the truth, the whole truth, and nothing but the truth. (Selectively, of course. We don't want any of that negative truth in there.)

Due to many people's inability to see themselves as they are, hypocrisy runs rampant in the world of online dating. I have spoken with innumerable women who have called me to complain about all the liars they end up meeting, yet they don't take any responsibility for lying in their own profiles. Their righteous indignation is priceless.

I had a woman call me at MatchNet to inform me that there was (gasp!) a liar on one of our websites. Shocked, I asked her what this awful man was lying about.

"His age," she said furiously. "He says he's forty-eight, but he's fifty. I know for a fact that he is fifty years old!" I did my duty and informed her that if she knows he's a liar, she probably shouldn't go out with him.

"You're just going to tolerate this?" she asked, incredulous at my passivity.

"Yes," I replied, before asking her why this man's two-year fib was of such great concern to her.

"He's my ex-husband," she screamed. "What are you going to do about him?!"

I told her that there was nothing I could do. "It's his right to misrepresent himself, just as it's your right to misrepresent yourself." Not surprisingly, this didn't satisfy her one bit. But really, you can't police liars online. You can only avoid them.

Then Again, a Half-Truth Can Go a Long Way

Briefly, I'm going to state a very unpopular opinion in defense of lying, using an anecdote from my friend Mitch. Mitch had been dating online for a few years, and the only long-term relationship he ever developed through the Internet started with a lie. He was twenty-seven. She was twenty-nine. She wrote to him. He wrote back. After a week of emailing and a week on the phone, they were head over heels about each other. Another two weeks into their budding relationship, and only minutes after they had slept together for the first time, this woman tells him that she has something she has to tell him. My buddy, Mr. Neurotic, starts thinking a mile a minute: AIDS, herpes, boyfriend, husband—until she finally spills the beans. "I'm not really twenty-nine. I'm thirty-one."

Mitch started laughing. His girlfriend was confused because, in her experience, a lot of men don't want to date women over thirty. And since Mitch was younger, she was worried that he might be freaked out by her true age. Actually, he couldn't have cared less. He liked her a lot. What did it matter if she was born in 1972 instead of 1974?

Now granted, not everyone will react as Mitch did, and not all lies are little white lies. But if a fifty-two-year-old woman recognizes that most men don't search for women over the age of fifty, I see no problem with her lowering her age to fifty so she can appear in his search, as long as she's honest later in the profile, or shortly thereafter on the phone. One may lie to open a door, as illustrated above, or one can lie to be deceitful. Personally, I think they are two very different things. Lying with a picture is also particularly common in the world of Internet dating—a subject that will be broached in Chapter Six.

Liars are an unfortunate peril of dating online, but all you can do is hold up your end of the bargain. You don't want liars on the Internet? Great. Don't lie.

"Inteligance is Definately Impotent to Me. I Like to Laff Alot. Oh, And Theirs Nothing Worse Than a Lier."

And I'm moving on to the next profile. I understand that not everyone is a Rhodes scholar, a walking dictionary, or an English professor, but honestly, people, your profile is all that anybody knows about you. Why advertise off the bat that you're indifferent, careless, and/or illiterate? If you were hunting for a job, you would never send out a résumé with spelling mistakes and grammatical errors. You'd probably reread it a dozen times, put it down, reread it again, and then finally give it to your two best friends to read a few more times, just in case you missed something. I urge you to do that with your profile. It can only help. Why eliminate a potential partner because you keep confusing "their" and "there"?

In Summation: Essays, Important

If telling you to put extra emphasis on the essay portion of your profile is a crime, then cuff me, book me, and make me drop the soap in the prison shower. I can't stress enough that what makes the difference between someone who's successful and unsuccessful on these dating sites is the essays. You cannot put enough time and effort into them, and those who give them short shrift are only hurting their own chances.

Some people vehemently defend their brief essays: "If they want to know more, they can ask," or "I've already had six people respond to them." To which I respond, in all candor, "Yes, and those six people have also written indiscriminately to every other person on this website." Some essays are so short that no one could possibly be writing to them in response to their wit, intelligence, or charm. Generally, I'll follow up by telling people that they probably are witty, intelligent, and charming—they just neglected to show it. So, please, show it! For your own good!

Oh, and while it should go without saying, I'll say it anyway: don't reveal any personal information in your profile, such as your real first and last name, your real email address, or your real ICQ or IM name. A lot of people like to cheat the online dating services and try to get around paying by putting their private information online. First of all, this is against every site's policies, and second of all, you're taking a security risk by giving out your personal information. I always like to assume that people are well intentioned, but all it takes is one bad apple writing nasty emails to ruin your whole Internet dating experience. Save the private stuff for later, okay?

A Dictionary for Online Personal Ads

The following is a copy of an email, once forwarded to me, that subtly suggests how what you read isn't always what you get in person.

Okay, so it's not so subtle.

WOMEN'S ADS

Adventurer .... Slept with all your friends

Average looking .... Has a face like a basset hound

Beautiful .... Pathological liar

Emotionally secure.. Medicated

40-ish 49

Friendship first .... Trying to live down reputation as a slut

Fun .... Annoying

Good listener .... Borderline autistic

New Age... All body hair, all the time

Old-fashioned .... Lights out, missionary position only

Open-minded .... Desperate

Outgoing .... Loud and embarrassing

Passionate .... Sloppy drunk

Poet .... Depressive schizophrenic

Professional .... Certified bitch

Romantic .... Looks better by candlelight

Rubenesque .... Fat

Voluptuous .... Very fat

Wants soul mate .... Stalker

Young at heart.. Old bat

MEN'S ADS

40-ish	52 and looking for 25-year-old
Athletic	Watches a lot of NASCAR
Average looking	Unusual hair growth on ears, nose, and back
Educated	Will patronize the shit out of you
Free spirit	Banging your sister
Friendship first	As long as friendship involves nookie
Fun	Good with a remote and a six-pack
Good-looking	Arrogant
Very good looking	Dumb as a board
Honest	Pathological liar
Huggable	Overweight, more body hair than a bear
Likes to cuddle	Insecure mama's boy
Mature	Older than your father
Open-minded	Wants to sleep with your roommate
Physically fit	Does a lot of 12-ounce Budweiser curls
Poet	Wrote ex-girlfriend's number on a bathroom stall
Sensitive	Cries at chick flicks
Spiritual	Got laid in a cemetery once
Stable	Arrested for stalking but not convicted
Thoughtful	Says "Excuse me" after he farts

"THINK CAROL AND MIKE BRADY WITHOUT THE FLIP HAIRDO OR THE AFRO."

CHAPTER 5

Analyzing Five Superb Internet Dating Profiles and Why They Work

When consulting with Internet daters, I take great pains to try to help people spruce up their profiles. There are usually a bunch of things that can be altered, but most folks have a large blind spot when it comes to writing about themselves honestly, objectively, and eloquently. Not only that, but very often the most articulate online daters write whatever comes out of their hearts without thinking of the effect their words are going to have on the reader.

In this chapter I have deconstructed five different profiles and attempted to analyze why I think they succeed. I took examples from all different demographics, men and women, twenties to sixties, to illustrate that as long as a person writes with a distinct voice the content can vary, but the result will still be positive. What works for one person does not necessarily work for everybody, but the general principles remain the same.

Use specifics. Be sincere and honest. Write like you talk. Show your personality. If you make jokes, make them tasteful, self-deprecating, or sarcastic, and do so with caution. Figure out what makes you different from everyone else, and use it to your advantage. Again, stay away from generic adjectives and focus more on proper nouns and stories. If you're going to be wordy, have something interesting to say. Stay consistently positive and confident without seeming annoying and arrogant. Be proud of who you are and wear it confidently in your language and tone. Don't give anyone a reason to say no to you. No red flags, no obvious baggage, no glaring insecurities, no diatribes about past relationships, no spelling mistakes, no superficial wish list about money or looks.

You should have fun writing your profile. If you have fun writing it, the reader will likely have fun reading it. Below are five people that I'd like to meet:

Username: MadamImadam
Headline: Not for the Palindromophobic
Vitals: Male, 28, Alexandria, VA

About Me . . . .
I know they say never to talk politics, but I'm afraid that would be virtually impossible. I'm an aide to a prominent senator from my home state in the Midwest, and while my life isn't my job, sometimes you might have to remind me. Fortunately, after six years in D.C., I've got a firm grasp on what's important. My friends out here are my substitute family, and, for better or worse, most of my substitute family is made up of lawyers like me. Through my involvement in a nonprofit organization called Turning the Page, I've been able to meet some amazing people who also care about the literacy problem in the inner city. Oh, God, I'm sounding like a Beltway insider—somebody stop me! Back before my days of blue suits and sixty-hour weeks, I was an elementary school spelling bee champ (up until the "spagheti" incident, that is), a college soccer player, and a Georgetown Law graduate. Because I'm the youngest of three, I was raised on classic rock (Led Zeppelin, Pink Floyd, The Beatles), so forgive me if I'm not quite the urban hipster. I can, however, play guitar and can cover pretty much any popular song prior to 1990. And, yes, I do take requests.

About the One I'm Looking For . . . .
I want an opposite. A yin to my yang, a Laurel to my Hardy, a Hall to my Oates. You provide balance in my life—a joie de vivre, a je ne sais quoi, perhaps even a croissant—that is currently lacking. I'll provide the corny French jokes. You're up on current events, but you don't sleep,

eat, and breathe it. You come from a close family, have a tremendously high sense of self-worth, and you handle yourself like a champ at parties. You bike through Rock Creek Park, you play in a coed softball league, and you can wield a paintball gun like Rambo—but it's all about fun first and exercise second. You are mature for your age and know what you want out of life, but you're not above a splash fight when rowing on the Potomac River on a sunny Sunday afternoon. And you won't get pissed at me when I show no mercy in soaking you to the bone, because one kiss from me makes it all better.

My Idea of Our Perfect First Date . . . .
Mr. Smith's in Georgetown. I order the French onion soup and the filet mignon. You order the Wineburger for $999—it's an eight-ounce patty with lettuce, tomatoes, and onions that comes with a $990 bottle of 1933 Chateau Lafite Rothschild. We clink glasses and don't stop talking until the lights are turned on and we're being escorted out the door.

My Perception of an Ideal Relationship . . . .
You are levelheaded, logical, and can put me in my place when I get all Type-A male, but you don't get bent out of shape that easily. You know that there are bumps in the road, but that the road is far preferable to the alternative. We are each other's mutual admiration society, where we talk just as glowingly behind each other's backs as we do to each other's faces. We give space when necessary and support when needed. And we both realize that when the initial sparks fade, what we're left with in the end is a special friendship that can last a lifetime.

What I've Learned from Past Relationships . . . .
Be open to new ideas because people can change. Give because you want to give, not because you're hoping to receive. A well-written card lasts a lot longer than a fancy dinner. Not everyone in D.C. is a boring stuffed-suit. I love being in love, and I'll never again settle for less.

Right off the bat, this guy let's you know that he's bright by using "Not for the Palindromophobic" as a headline. This is a good strategy if he's looking to attract a woman of similar intelligence. Like a good politician, he tries to appeal to multiple constituencies, citing his Midwestern roots, his love of family, his high-profile job, and his involvement in charity work. This isn't manipulative; it's smart. He exhibits some necessary self-awareness when he starts sounding too "D.C." and immediately apologizes for it. This is also disarming because it allows him to continue like this with a reader's permission because he's acknowledged his flaw. Throwing in his past as an athlete and musician is vital to broadening his appeal as a well-rounded young man. The specifics of his second essay make for really breezy reading and establish him as a person with whom a woman can have fun. By citing the "Wineburger," he hints that he may be generous and romantic, two qualities that are universally attractive. His final two essays show him to be not just glib but relationship-oriented and mature, with an eye towards the future.

Username: 1in6Billion
Headline: A Barrel of Monkeys Has Nothing on Me
Vitals: Female, 35, Boston, MA

About Me. . . . .
Weird things happen to me; nothing that you should be afraid of, but just realize that if we get together, you're in for a wild ride. I've driven a go-kart for six laps with the back of the car in flames. My VW has broken down in front of a dozen honking customers in the drive-thru line at McDonald's (I've since upgraded to a better model). I work in public relations. I spend my days getting press coverage for people in the film and television industries, but the truth is, I'd rather be making my own headlines. My ultimate goal is to move to Los Angeles to be a writer/producer of feature films. Storytelling is my passion, but it won't be easy to leave my family behind because they are my anchor and the paradigm of everything that I aspire to be. I'm fortunate to have them in my life, not to mention a legion of close friends from high school and college. I'm pragmatic but spontaneous. Nurturing but competitive. Peaceful but energetic. I love staying up late—whether it's to party, have sex, or just read a good book—but I almost always sleep in on weekends. I definitely have an adventurous streak—whether it's trying out an exotic recipe in the kitchen, running with my dog, or traveling the world thanks to my good friends at Orbitz and Priceline. My dream trip is taking the Orient Express from Paris to Venice to Budapest, then relaxing on a Greek island with nothing but sunscreen, James Patterson books, and *InStyle* magazine. Are you in?

About the One I'm Looking For. . . . .

I'd rather be with a guy who has big dreams and no money than a guy with no dreams and big money. I must admit, I like a bit of a bad boy—not an awful, I'm-going-to-treat-you-like-crap kind of guy—but someone who's going to push me to my limits and then pull back with a warm hug at the last minute. Truth is, I'm just a nice girl (most of the time) who's looking for some fun and companionship (not necessarily in that order). I love funny guys who can hold me spellbound with a story or make me laugh until I cry. I also love creativity and passion. Maybe it's your love of '80s movies, your baseball card collection, or the fact that you moved across country with only a duffel bag—it doesn't matter. The right man not only fascinates me but also brings out the best in me. We push each other to be the greatest people we can be. We bolster each other's egos and we leave short, thoughtful love messages for each other when we're away on business trips. If you're comfortable in your own skin, have a strong sense of self, and aren't afraid to expose your flaws, I'm sure we'll get along just fine. But I will say that if you've got blue eyes, are a Red Sox fan, or a part-time singer/guitarist, I'm already melting.

My Idea of Our Perfect First Date . . . .

We've built up such chemistry on the phone that when I open the door and see you, I grab you by the back of the neck and kiss you before we even leave the house. (Note: Don't you DARE try this—some fantasies are best left as fantasies.)

My Perception of an Ideal Relationship . . . .

Complete and utter comfort. I can be myself around you without feeling judged. You can sit in your room working while I do a crossword and I'm entirely content. I only have eyes for you, you only have eyes for me, and we communicate this verbally, physically, and often. Down and dirty sex and warm and comforting cuddling are ever present. Fights are rare and when we do get into it, we don't stop talking until we've reached some sort of peace. Unparalleled companionship, unprecedented generosity, and unconditional love grant us the foundation for a lasting long-term relationship.

What I've Learned from Past Relationships. . . . .

Flossing is important. Laughing is essential. Perfection is impossible. Better to be single than to be in a bad relationship. If it's worth it, I'll work for it; if it's not, I won't. Don't say anything you'll regret because you can't take it back. Finally, you must expose yourself emotionally—it's the only way to reap love's greatest rewards.

lin6Billion's essays scream out: fun! Leading with a pair of *I Love Lucy* type anecdotes is a smart move because it immediately captures the reader's attention and establishes that this is a woman who knows how to laugh at herself. Such funny stories are also a logical lead-in to her career goal of being a Hollywood writer. Her high aspirations, however, are tempered by her down-to-earth nature and her attachment to her family. Great use of specifics in the last line of her "About Me" essay, which describes an adventuresome person looking for someone to share the ride. What comes across clearly is that she's looking for more of an equal than an opposite. Just as the author describes herself as creative, a dreamer, and an adventurer, she suggests that her ideal man should be like-minded. Little touches round out her second essay—baseball cards, love messages on business trips, part-time guitarist. Using the word "melting" shows a hint of vulnerability and a flair for the romantic as well. While she pushes the sexual envelope in her subsequent essays, she also expresses a deep wisdom and maturity about what it takes to sustain a long-term relationship. Overall, she would appear to be a woman who has experienced a lot in life and is open to all forms of excitement and happiness.

Username: PowerNerd

Headline: Objects in This Mirror Are Not As Dorky As They Might Appear

Vitals: Male, 43, Bloomington, IN

About Me. . . . .
Once you get past the self-deprecating humor, you will soon learn that I'm a raging egomaniac. Nah, that's not true, either. How do you just say that you're a nice, successful guy looking to share his life with his future soul mate? I guess that would do it. I'm the proud dad of a six-year-old boy and a four-year-old girl, and my wife and I have been amicably divorced for a year now. I'm past the breakup and excited to meet some good people on here. Friendship is not at all out of the question. It's welcomed. My business isn't glamorous—I own my own web design firm—

but it is lucrative, and I love the challenge of running my own company. I'm not married to my work, and even when I was actually married, I found time for tae kwon do (yes, nice guys can kick ass!), classic movies (you MUST see *Sunset Boulevard* and *The Philadelphia Story* if you haven't yet), and the occasional fishing excursion (nothing like a little time alone to recharge your batteries). Things are different now, but I look forward to taking some chances and seeing who's out there.

About the One I'm Looking For. . . . .
I smile when I think of you. I walk down College Avenue and I want to buy you a $400 purse that you pointed out but would never get for yourself. You like my kids. You put up with my mom. (She means well; really, she does!) You fawn over me, cook me dinner, massage me before bed, and have a highly developed sense of sarcasm. I think it's cute when you snort as you laugh. You make fun of me when I can't leave the house without forgetting my cell phone. You act younger than you look because I like mature women who haven't forgotten what it's like to be a girl.

My Idea of Our Perfect First Date . . . .
It doesn't involve a chain restaurant, a roller coaster, or a movie. It may involve eating, excitement, or entertainment. It definitely involves me, you, and a long, drawn-out moment where we don't want to say good night.

My Perception of an Ideal Relationship . . . .
After a ten-year relationship, I may be rusty about this courting stuff, but I'm not jaded by divorce. It's even clearer to me that there's not just one person out there. And even if you get lucky and meet a winner, there's a mountain of work ahead, no matter what. It's knowing that the work is worth it, that the whole is greater than the sum of its parts, which redeems the institution of marriage. I'm not looking to jump into anything, but I'm a firm believer in chemistry and wouldn't turn my back on someone incredible just because I'm recently single. A perfect relationship is one in which the reality is not that far from your fantasy. As long as you have a realistic fantasy, you are bound to one day find your bliss.

What I've Learned from Past Relationships. . . . .
It's better to understand than to be understood. Laughter can save a relationship; lack of laughter can kill it. Having kids makes you a better person, but it will also complicate your marriage in ways impossible to

understand from the outside. The Hoosiers will tear your heart out, but it's fun to have something outside yourself to root for together. Soup can actually be an aphrodisiac if served at the right time of night. And finally, this being-single thing isn't going to be nearly as bad as I thought it might be . . .

What PowerNerd does extraordinarily well is to remain extremely optimistic despite being a newly divorced father. You don't hear him talking about his awful ex-wife or his annoyance at the online dating process. In the first essay, he discusses finding a soul mate. In the fourth essay, he talks about the validity of marriage. In the fifth essay, he closes on a note of optimism as well. What's not to like about someone who has overcome such big obstacles and has maintained a smile in the process? Plus, he's a combination of humility—witness his headline—and assuredness, as shown by his career as an entrepreneur and a martial artist. Those touches, in addition to doses of humor about his forgetfulness, his meddling mother, and the sexual properties of soup, make him a genuine catch for any woman who is looking to settle down with a nice, normal, grounded man. Subtle use of details regarding his love of Indiana basketball, his willingness to give (a $400 purse?), and his occasional need for personal space add to the profile. Alternating tones between warmth and sarcasm doesn't feel like a contradiction as much as it seems to be the sign of a fully formed human being.

Username: NachoMama
Headline: Back in the Saddle Again
Vitals: Female, 57, Albuquerque, NM

About Me. . . . .
You know that woman who is the first person on the dance floor at every party? That's me. Music is in my soul and also in my blood. My Dad was a guitarist who played sessions with Clapton and Hendrix, and while I haven't inherited his talent, I have inherited his passion, his rhythm, and his ranch. I live in Loma del Rey near Hoffman Park with my two German Shepherds, Poodle and Chow (yes, I have a goofy sense of humor). My husband of thirty-two years passed away three years ago, and while there's a strange freedom in being single, there's a big void as well. My three children (two doctors and an artist—I have

to brag!) are spread out around the country, so I've learned to make the best of my new life. I retired from teaching high school Spanish in 2001 and, thanks to my pension, get to travel considerably more than I did when I was working. Last year, I took a road trip to visit friends on the West Coast, and later I spent three weeks roughing it all around New Zealand with a girlfriend. I'm a Catholic of Mexican heritage, and while it's a big part of my identity, it doesn't have to be a part of yours. A big heart, a big smile, and a big . . . car (to travel in, of course!) are all that I require from a man.

About the One I'm Looking For. . . . .

At this stage in my life, I'm not at all demanding. I just know what I want. Someone widowed, as opposed to someone divorced—no bias against the divorcés out there, but there's a basic unspoken understanding among surviving spouses that is hard to explain. I'm not a money-grubber, but it would be great if you were successful, because, as I've said, I live comfortably and do enjoy seeing the world. Maybe it's my background, but, despite my occasionally bawdy mouth and sometimes off-color mind, I'm a traditionalist at heart. Family is everything to me. Hopefully, our worlds will mesh seamlessly. Think Carol and Mike Brady, without the flip hairdo or the afro.

My Idea of Our Perfect First Date . . . .

It's a warm night. You pick me up at my house. I'm wearing a sundress even though there's no sun. You compliment me and I blush demurely. Being a gentleman, you open the car door and take me to a restaurant. Being an extraordinary gentleman, you remember from my profile that I like Italian food (must be a hot-blooded thing). We end up at a table for two, lit by a lone candle. A bottle of Cab, a linguine with clam sauce, and a chicken scarpariello later, we're gazing at each other's eyes over a cup of cappuccino, wondering how we could live so close without ever meeting before.

My Perception of an Ideal Relationship . . . .

Mutual love of salsa dancing, **Marx Brothers** movies, *West Side Story*, Machu Picchu, Diego Rivera, John Irving, Barbara Kingsolver, yoga, mint chocolate chip ice cream, and, of course, my doggies.

What I've Learned from Past Relationships

Some acknowledged clichés: Make every day count. Work like you don't need the money, love like you've never been hurt, and dance like no one is watching. People don't change. I can compromise, but, at my age, I am who I am, and if we're not a fit, that's okay. Remembering why you fell in love originally is a great way to make that love come rushing back. Life will always knock you down—it's how quickly you get up that is the measure of your character. Be open to the unexpected. Odds are that's where the richest pleasures will come from.

Articulate, funny, vibrant, interesting . . . NachoMama has it all. I love her opening line, because with a single image, she has said so much about her personality. A reader could rightfully infer that the first to get up and dance is a passionate woman who takes life by the horns and doesn't care what the people on the sidelines are thinking. She has an incredible use of specifics. In that first essay alone, we learn that she's a retired teacher, a healed widow, a proud mother, a world traveler, and a good Catholic. Name-dropping Eric Clapton never hurt anyone, but I was more struck by the silly names of her dogs. You have no doubt what you're getting when you write to this woman. Just as striking is her stringent criteria for the man she is looking for—widowers only. I think that this probably eliminates some decent men who may be empathetic to her widowhood, but at least she is up front about her needs and wants, which cuts down on unnecessary email exchanges. Her first date is lively and romantic, and her list of "mutual loves" is broad enough to attract all types of men.

Username: FatherTime

Headline: Takes a Licking . . .

Vitals: Male, 65, Aventura, FL

About Me . . . .

I'm sixty-five going on twenty-five, but apparently I'm senile enough to have my username suggest that I'm the oldest man on Earth. That's not quite true, although I remember the Korean War more vividly than I remember the recent war in Iraq. (There was a war, wasn't there?) I don't want to suggest that I live in a time warp. Being a father and grandfather forces me to keep current or risk obsolescence, or worse, mockery. So while I might be partial to Johnny Mathis, I'm at least aware of Eminem, and that puts me over the top with my young ones.

I was a chemical engineer for Glaxo Pharmaceuticals for thirty years and retired to the steam-room-like conditions of Florida five years ago. The weather makes a full round of golf turn into a full aerobic workout, so while my scores are suffering, my waistline is shrinking as well. I was once happily married and have always longed to get that feeling back again. Guess that's why I'm here. I don't have double standards and take great pride in being a gentleman—picking up the check, walking you to your front door, laying my coat down over a puddle just like Sir Walter Raleigh. Last time I was dating regularly, there was no Internet (and no color TV), so forgive me if I can't immediately send a picture. My grandson will probably help me scan one if I give him five bucks or something. It's still cheaper than Kinko's, isn't it?

About the One I'm Looking For. . . . .

All class, all the time. You can tell your salad fork from your dinner fork. You don't take it as an insult when I open your car door for you. You know Lincoln Center from the Lincoln Memorial, and you've been to both. I wouldn't say that my standards are any higher than anyone else's—they're just my own. I'm the rare man who thinks that trophy wives make men look worse rather than better, so you're probably of the same generation as I am. The more we have in common, the better. Do you prefer the Seychelles to Sea World? Arnaz to Diaz? Red wine to white? If so, we're on the right track, and I'm looking forward to getting to know you further.

My Idea of Our Perfect First Date . . . .

Dinner at an outdoor bistro on the water at sundown. Simple, elegant, comfortable. The rest is about the company. I promise to not only hold up my end of the conversation but to pick up the tab as well.

My Perception of an Ideal Relationship . . . .

I will spend the rest of my life with you and never get bored. I cherish your opinions on the latest foreign policy debacle, stem cell research, and my crazy brother Ted. You can dazzle me with a smile, you can calm me with a kiss, you can make me swoon with a poem. I can whip up apple pie à la mode from scratch (okay, not the mode, but the pie), I can massage you like a pro after a long, hard day of golf, I can make you giggle with a funny face. Growing older doesn't mean growing more serious—it means growing sillier because you care less and less what other people think.

What I've Learned from Past Relationships. . . . .

I've had lots of time to get better at being a good partner, and experience and wisdom are the best teachers. Long ago, I stopped "sweating the small stuff," because the big stuff puts it all into perspective. You'll be the beneficiary of that—a kinder, gentler FatherTime, if you will. We should talk things out without raising our voices, and we should remember to separate our feelings from our issues, so that disagreements don't escalate unnecessarily. I take great enjoyment out of being generous. Giving is better than receiving if you're giving it to someone you love.

We can't tell what age bracket FatherTime is trying to attract. He hedges his bets in acknowledging his real age but also makes reference to keeping current. If he wants to date a woman ten or more years younger than he is, this is a good tactic. Simply mentioning Johnny Mathis is brilliant, because I know from my parents that Mathis equals romance, and who doesn't appreciate a little romance? He maintains a good, detached sense of humor throughout—joking about his age, about the Florida humidity, about his inability to scan a picture—but he never sounds like he's trying too hard to be funny. Cultural references establish his character (perhaps a history maven or a TV trivia buff) but don't overwhelm the essays. He leaves little doubt to a potential mate that he's going to be an excellent companion—witty, thoughtful, gentlemanly, wise. Despite his divorced status, I wouldn't once wonder whether this man can maintain a successful monogamous relationship—he's way too sincere and easygoing to be a player.

"THAT'S YOU?!"

CHAPTER 6

On Why a Picture Is Worth at Least 250 Words (and Probably More)

An oft-cited statistic from my former employers at Matchnet is that members who posted photos received eight times more responses than members who didn't post photos.

Are you kidding me?

My guess is that members with photos get *fifty-eight* times more responses. Match.com reports that "guys are 14 times more likely to look at a profile with a photo; women are 8.5 times more likely to check out your profile if you have a photo; and members with photos get contacted seven times more often than members without."

Now remember, I'm the guy who's sitting here stressing the importance of strong essays. And although I'd like to think that I've got an ounce of depth, who are we kidding? Pictures are the single-most important thing to a viewer checking out your profile.

Working as a consultant for MatchNet, talking to people all over America, I found the contact logs of the male and female members to be remarkable. Everybody wrote to the same forty beautiful people. Thus, you can't overestimate the importance of a good picture. It's the first thing you see, it's what draws you in, and, as anyone with any libido and Internet dating experience already knows, it's what often makes you fire off a "Hi, Beautiful" email even before you have read the profile.

People who are not perfect specimens can take heart in the fact that the perfect specimens, because they have the option of going out with whomever they want on the website, will usually choose the other perfect specimens, thereby leaving everybody else open for the taking. Yes, it's true: attractive people, just like in real life, have far more online dating options than average-looking people. But average people have far more online dating options than unattractive people. And unattractive people have far more online dating options than people who don't have pictures up.

Anyway, if you're going to be the rebel who bucks the picture trend while resting on this futile defense, "if someone wants to get to know me, they can write to me!"—sorry, but you're wrong. They ain't gonna write to you.

They are going to write to the woman with the big boobs. They are going to write to the woman with the nice smile. They are going to write to the woman with the long red hair.

And you, my pictureless friend, will remain at the bottom of the online dating totem pole, where nobody can see you.

Five Immutable Rules About Posting Your Picture

I don't like to lay out hard-and-fast "rules" when it comes to my approach to online dating. After all, these are just my opinions— suggestions that I can make after years of dating and consulting experience. Ultimately, you have to feel comfortable putting up your picture for the world (or at least the Internet dating world) to see.

But when it comes to photos, there are rules that go beyond any debate—standards, that, if they are not adhered to, will completely undermine all the other hard work that you've done in reading this book. So pay close attention and, if necessary, use a highlighter. This stuff is important.

Put Up a Picture

Even if you are an awesome writer with a killer profile, you need to have a picture up. Photoless folk will hardly be contacted by anyone. So many people do have pictures up that there's little incentive to search through the profiles of those who don't. Think about it. If it all starts with attraction, the first and most obvious way to draw someone in is through a great picture. Those who insist (for privacy purposes) that they go without a picture do so at their own risk.

There are those who maintain that they simply cannot imagine being discovered by anyone they know seeing their face on the Internet. To these people, I say one thing: "If someone is looking at your picture on an online dating website, then, guess what? They're online dating themselves." In short, there's nothing to be embarrassed about. The perceived stigmas attached to online dating are gone. (And if they're not, boy, am I going to be embarrassed when this book turns into a best-seller and Oprah wants to interview me and I have to admit on national television that I'm an "expert" at online dating. How horrifying.)

You Knew There'd Be an Exception, Didn't You?

Now every once in a while, I'll talk with a person who, for some reason or another, just can't put up a picture. Fine, if you're a psychologist and you don't want your patients to get a window into your personal life, keeping your face off the Internet is understandable. If you're running for mayor of Cleveland and you already have a trophy wife to call your own, it may be a bad idea to post your face online. If you're Drew Barrymore and you're newly single, I'd have to guess there's a better outlet for you. But the rest of you people? Get with the program. Run down to a copy shop with a 4 x 6 glossy, get it scanned onto a floppy disk, and email it to the website of your choice. Better yet, email four pictures that show four different sides of you. You'll be glad that you did.

Put Up a Picture That Looks Like You Look Today (Even If You Looked Better Five Years Ago)

The single biggest complaint about Internet dating: "People don't look like their photos!" Hmm . . . and whose fault is that? Putting up a picture that is not representative of how you actually look is no different from lying about your annual income or about the existence of your recently separated husband. In fact, it's worse, because this is a lie you get busted on the second you open the door. Talk about self-sabotage. If you put up a picture that looks appreciably better than you, I can guarantee you that there will not be a second date, and, in all likelihood, the first one will probably suck too. It's hard to act all excited when you're sitting across from someone and all you're thinking is, "His profile did not say, 'Hair color: flesh.'"

Therefore, I implore you from the bottom of my heart: be honest with yourself. If you're a woman who, ten years and two babies ago, was a svelte 120 pounds, but now are a more womanly 145 pounds, you almost certainly used to like the way you looked better than you do now. The question is: are you going to put up that old picture of you in the halter top or the more realistic recent shot of you wearing a black evening gown for that "slimming" effect?

You know the bikini picture would get a better reaction than the gown, so say you decide to post it. Now, every guy who meets you is expecting to meet the woman in the bikini but, much to his immediate surprise, is meeting a very different looking woman. It's fair for him to be disappointed.

But Everybody Else Does It

Okay, let's reverse the roles. Let's say when you spoke to him, he said he was forty-seven, but now that you meet him, he confesses that he's actually a "very young" fifty-seven. Tell me you're not going to be searching for the nearest red exit sign, no matter how youthful this very nice liar may look.

You may think that you can overcome those little white lies about your physical appearance, but you can't. I don't care if you're as funny as Robin Williams. I don't care if you're as charming as James Bond. I don't care if so many sparks were flying on the phone you had to hang up to avoid injury. If your picture doesn't look at all like you, you're guilty of false advertising. And if I'm your date, I'm going to want my money back.

Put Up Only Good Pictures (Once Again, As Long As They Look Like You)

Pictures that are *not good:*

- Pictures taken at a three-minute photo booth in your local mall
- Pictures taken in your living room for the express purpose of putting them up on the web
- Pictures taken by a webcam on top of your computer
- Pictures taken at the DMV that you Xerox off of your license
- Pictures taken of you in a suit and tie for your company website
- Pictures taken more than five years ago
- Pictures taken more than four years ago
- Pictures taken more than three years ago
- Pictures taken more than two years ago
- Pictures taken with ex-boyfriends or ex-girlfriends
- Pictures taken that show too much skin—shirtless men, women in bikinis
- Pictures taken from too close-up
- Pictures taken from too far away
- Pictures taken where you're not smiling

- Pictures taken of a large group of people where you are just one small speck in the crowd

- Pictures taken out of focus

- Pictures taken in a dimly lit room.

- Pictures taken where something about you looks considerably different—your hair, your weight, whatever

- Pictures taken that are not of you but of a model you saw on the Internet

That's it. Other than that, you should be all set.

Put Up Pictures That Enhance and Reinforce What You Wrote in Your Profile

Most websites have multiple slots for pictures. Udate and Kiss offer three. AmericanSingles and JDate offer four. Matchmaker and Lavalife offer ten. Match offers twenty-six. BlackPlanet even lets you design your own web page. Regardless of the number, those pictures are the first things anyone looks at, so you ought to take them pretty seriously. If you're wondering what kind of pictures you can put up (given all the rules I listed previously), consider that the only pictures I've told you not to post are ones that are inappropriate, dishonest, or poor quality. That leaves everything else under the sun for you to play with.

I had a client at E-Cyrano named Stacy who spent a good deal of time talking about how important family and friends are to her in her essays. So, in addition to her primary photo (which is, she admits, one of the best pictures ever taken of her), she also has a picture of her with her mom, a picture of her with her friends at a wedding, and a picture of her with her roommate, dressed up for a night on the town.

You can look at these pictures and get a glimpse into Stacy's life. If you like what you see, she's confident she's going to hear back from you. As a former MatchNet colleague of mine used to say to customers, "Post pictures that make your life look like one that someone else would want to be a part of." In Stacy's photos, the warmth between her and her loved ones is readily apparent. She's smiling broadly in every single picture. This makes her profile all the more inviting to a total stranger.

By the way, four pictures aren't necessary for every profile, as scanning can be expensive (up to ten dollars per picture). Many people put up two quality photos—a recent close-up and a full-body shot—that show your suitors everything they need to see. People tend to have a litany of excuses as to why they don't have any pictures posted, from "I have no good pictures of myself" to "I don't have a digital camera" to "I don't have any way to post my photos online." I don't buy any of these excuses because the Rx is far too simple: a disposable camera, a one-hour photo, and a cheap scanner. Scanners cost as little as fifty dollars, and they're incredibly easy to use. Get one. It's a smart investment.

Ignore the Cliché: You Are Not What You Eat, But What You DO!

If you find that your life is more defined by your activities or possessions, it makes it a lot easier to post some cool pictures. You love to ride your Harley? Let's see you straddling that big chrome hog. Big-time scuba diver? A photo of you in a wet suit will show off your interests as well as your pecs. Are you a proud grandma? Bring out the drooling tykes and place 'em on your lap. Love your poodle to death? Let's see Bobo in his white, fluffy splendor, licking your face affectionately. If costume parties are your thing, let's see you and your buddies dressed as the Village People. Don't be shy. This is who you are! Embrace it. Flaunt it. A person captivated by your fun, interesting, smiling pictures is more than likely to respond to your profile—yes, I will admit—even if your essays are subpar.

There's no accounting for superficiality, whether we like it or not. Pretty people will always have a considerable amount of online options, but they can make themselves even more inviting and approachable by posting pictures and writing essays that show their deeper side. Many women coast by on their looks alone and wonder why all they seem to get are losers.

Well, think about it this way: any loser can be bold enough to hit on a gorgeous stranger when he doesn't have to approach her in person. He can edit his introductory letter for an hour if he likes, while in real life he generally won't be given an hour to come up with a suave pick-up line. Unfortunately, despite the inherent advantages of being able to choose your words wisely in introducing yourself to the online supermodels, most people go with the standard "Hey, you look cute" approach, which has quickly replaced "What's your sign?" for opening line supremacy. It just doesn't work. But that's another topic for another chapter.

Finally . . . Smile!!!

Unless you have no teeth, SMILE! People like happy people. Yes, always.

Your pictures are nothing less than the gateway to your online dating success. They may not seal the deal entirely, but good photos are a virtual prerequisite to kicking open the door to meet that special someone.

Now start kicking!

"I'm Sorry, but There Were a Tremendous Number of Qualified Applicants for This Position."

Internet dating is a double-edged sword for women. For while, as a woman, you may sit at the top of the online pyramid, picking and choosing from a considerable number of suitors, men don't understand what it's like to be you.

I do. Not from any personal experience, but I've talked to enough exasperated women to know that it's no pleasure cruise being inundated with email from total strangers.

And if you're an attractive actress in her thirties, like one of my clients, Jamie, you've got literally hundreds (to thousands) of men responding to your profile based on your picture alone. Men of more depth may read what you wrote. Unfortunately, there aren't all that many men of depth. As a result, you spend your first four days on Site X checking out all the men who wrote to you—the vast majority of whom you wouldn't go out with in a million years. Hey, a woman's got to have her standards. Most of the emails you receive will tend to be long and fawning or short and crude. Here is one email that manages to achieve the rare combination of being both long and crude. A female friend who, to her credit, has learned not to take the vulgarians too seriously forwarded it to me.

Dear Nancy,

I love the softness and immenseness of your breasts . . . the zest of woman . . . I dream of moving man hands up and down your body . . . fully erected . . . exploring your curvature . . . all while moving around inside you . . . exploding then . . . making you moan and moan and moan and explode then yourself . . . I would caress your tits . . . fondle them wherever we walked . . . elevator, gardens, on the back of the boat, would have sex with you in public bathroom . . . in classrooms . . . on the bus . . . caressing your tits . . .

Sasha

Honestly, that letter, in its broken English, made me laugh until I cried, but it's a prime example of the filth that women have to put up with. It's disgusting and altogether too common, and it's the type of thing that gives Internet dating a bad rap. The "authors" of such emails are harmless—they're undoubtedly the same men who invented the catcall and whistle as a pick-up tool—but it would be easy to see why a sophisticated and attractive woman might not want to subject herself to stuff like this.

The Ironic Problem of Being an Attractive Woman on the Internet

I'm not saying we should shed any tears for gorgeous women, any more than we should pity the celebrities who get hounded for autographs, but certain people get flooded by so many responses that, at a certain point, they shut off and start deleting mail from their inbox without even reading it. The next thing you know, they've given up on Internet dating entirely and have determined that online people are weirdos. That's not fair. Take two hundred random men out at a bar on a given night, and you'll find a good percentage are weirdos, too. It's just too bad that women become the equivalent of online celebrities, when all they're looking to do is find someone nice and normal who doesn't just value them for their looks. That's why so many quit after only a few days of online dating.

But your best friend met her husband on this site. And another girlfriend is getting serious with an Internet guy. So you really believe in the concept of Internet dating, but you just don't want to deal with the riffraff such as "The Caresser" from before. What's a girl who wants to be valued for more than just her face to do?

A Radical Solution That Will Knock Your Manolos Off

I know this may sound a little wacky, but you may want to take down your pictures. Voilá. Problem solved. With no photo, no one can be obsessed with how you look. This approach puts you firmly in the driver's seat. You may be wondering what kind of response rate you'll get without any pictures. The answer? Virtually none. But, by hiding one of your greatest assets, you have just weeded out almost all men, since they usually don't even look at women without pictures. What about the ones who do write to little ol' pictureless you? Well, it's either some guy who fires off an email to anyone who checks off "female," or it may be that rare man of substance who bothered to respond to your essays despite the lack of photos. It's easy to tell the difference between the two.

Don't get me wrong: it's worth your while to see what it's like to put up pictures, but don't think that taking them down has to mean the end of your Internet dating experience. For some women (especially the best-looking ones), it may be wisest to not have any pictures up at all. The ego boost of getting letters from around the globe is easily offset by the massive time commitment it takes to look up everyone who writes to you. If you value yourself as more than a pretty face and can articulate that in your profile, you'll now have men who want to meet you for who you are, not for how you look. Isn't that refreshing? At the very least, it's superior to the bar scene, where you can't stand alone for ten seconds without an offer to buy you a drink.

This new approach, however, puts the onus upon you to do two things really well: write great essays and be proactive. If no one is writing to you because you can't be seen (and you are virtually invisible without a picture), then you have to write to who you think is smart and handsome and funny. And if you're going to write to him, and he can't see what you look like, you better have a memorable profile. The kind of profile that's going to make a man write back, "Wow! You sound amazing! Can I see a picture of you?" Upon which you email him a scanned photo of yourself, and he will thank the good Lord above for smiling upon him and blessing him with this woman who he probably thought was way out of his league. The only two serious Internet girlfriends I've ever had didn't have any pictures up, but their profiles were intriguing enough for me to respond to their initial emails. When I saw their respective photos, fuhgeddaboutit. I was hooked.

Oh, and so as not to leave half the population out, just be aware that there are fewer men out there who can get away with not writing to others. It makes sense. The women are too busy sifting through the legions of guys who have already contacted them first.

"TO BUY OR NOT TO BUY, IT'S NOT EVEN A QUESTION."

CHAPTER 7

Why Men Should Write to Women, Women Should Write to Men, and Everyone Should Buy a One-Year Subscription

The natural inclination for most people is to do the least possible work and hope for the best results. Well, by virtue of reading this far, I'm guessing you've already overcome that obstacle. Clearly you want to have a great experience using the Internet as a dating tool. Good. I want you to, as well. So stick with me while I go off on a bit of a tangent, okay?

Ask yourself this question. How often do you fall in love? Once a year? Once every five years? Once in your lifetime? Face it, dating isn't easy, and finding someone who makes you want to stop dating is even tougher. Internet dating companies would love to guarantee that each and every one of us will be engaged in the next year, but that wouldn't be true. More realistically, you'll meet some people, go on some dates, and, if they don't work out, meet some more people and go on some more dates. Over and over again, you'll keep on dating until you've found your soul mate. That person is online, or, if not there now, he or she may be in six months. That's why you can't give up when using the web to meet people. If the goal is to find your one and only, you have to give yourself the best chance to do so, which means taking your time and not getting frustrated if it doesn't happen overnight.

What's the Rush?

Conventional online dating wisdom says: write to as many members as possible in one month, and if you go on five coffee dates a week, maybe you'll find someone with whom you'll "click." Wait, wait, wait. First of all, you've already acknowledged that it's hard to fall in love, so why are you giving yourself only one month to do it? You know and I know that you're lucky if you fall in love this year. So get a longer subscription or more credits when you initially sign up. This saves you a good amount of money off the bat, and on most sites it also locks you in at a lower renewal rate if you choose to go month-by-month in the future. In a perfect world, you'd fall in love on your first date and you would have way overspent. But if this were a perfect world, you wouldn't be online dating at all. It's wise to step back and realize that you're probably going to stick around until you find Mr./Ms. Right, however long it may take. If getting married while you still have five months remaining on a site is your biggest problem, you should consider yourself the luckiest person in the world.

Once Bitten, Twice Shy

The typical Internet dater who is consistently meeting people on a site will usually stay active until finding a boyfriend/girlfriend. Yahoo reports that members stay for an average of three to six months before canceling and that 25 percent of users return in the future. While erratic, the patterns are there. I've seen them up close. Two months online, one month off. Three months online. Find a boyfriend. Break up. Get back on for one month. People who don't find love will often quit due to lack of results, but rarely do they question why things didn't work out for them. Most people just don't want to take a good hard look in the mirror.

It's Easy to Blame Everybody Else

There's always something that can be improved in your profile. If it's not your pictures and it's not your essays (although it often is), it may be your whole approach to Internet dating that undermines you. A man may sign up for a month and write to six hundred women, "You and me, babe, how about it?" and be baffled that no one writes him back. A woman may target one man whom she signed up just to meet, and if he doesn't write her back, she'll be so devastated that she'll never use the site again. Both scenarios are common because they play to our natural inclination to take the easy way out. To cut and paste one sentence into six hundred emails doesn't take any work. To quit after one rejection doesn't take any work. And in the end, the only people who really lose are the ones who quit before finding someone. As stated in an old New York State lottery ad, "You've gotta be in it to win it." Patience (and honesty) are the most important virtues when dating online.

"Fiddler on the Roof" Got It Wrong— Screw Tradition

You can probably tell that I feel that you're missing out on the fun of Internet dating if you're not a paid subscriber. A few sites like AmericanSingles and Nerve allow you to sit back and wait for people to contact you so that you can respond to them for free, which is okay if people are writing to you. Paying for a subscription or for credits allows you to initiate contact with other members (and respond to other members, which you usually can't do without paying). To me, the whole point of this online dating thing is to give you the freedom of choice. You can browse and browse and browse and then go, "Ooooh, he's hot!" And then, if you're a paid subscriber, you can write to him. If not, you have to pray that he writes to you first.

Allow me to take a few steps back and get some definitions straight. First: "member." Most websites will consider you a "member" just by virtue of your putting up a profile. Membership generally entitles you to browse all the profiles on the site and receive emails either at home or at the website's online mailbox. "Subscribers" are the ones who pay. Some women prefer to be members and not paid subscribers. This has half to do with fear of rejection and half to do with tradition.

Tradition is a delightful anachronism, but basking in the glow of it is counterproductive. The rules have changed. Women who write to men aren't "aggressive" or "desperate." They're smart. You want something, you go and get it. You snooze, you lose. There is a huge misconception among women who date online that "if he's interested in me, he'll write to me first." Uh uh. Not necessarily. Here's why.

Most websites have a function in which, while searching, you can tag an attractive or interesting member as a favorite. At the MatchNet sites, there were hot lists. At Lavalife, there were stars. At Matchmaker, there were peaches and trophies and flames that read "hot." All of these markers are designed to save you the trouble of sifting through hundreds of members every time you log on to the website. Well, let's say that when Jim gets started, he goes through five hundred women's profiles in a few hours. I know Jim and he is selective, but in all probability he's going to find a good thirty women who are appealing to him. Some people find more, some people find fewer, but there's generally enough talent out there on any given website to warrant a subscription purchase.

When Your Cup Runneth Over

Let's suppose that after signing up, Jim lists thirty women as his favorites, and then writes thoughtful, personal, funny emails to his ten favorites. And let's suppose that three of those women are incredibly flattered and write back. Let's also suppose that because Jim put up five pictures and wrote a creative, articulate profile that an interesting woman who has a subscription has written to him. Now he's juggling four women. His plate is full. Maybe it will take more than ten letters to get three responses, but the point is that an active Internet dater will generally end up with a few things brewing in his/her love life at once.

Now, let's add in the factor that there are new women joining the site all the time, and while Jim is casually dating four women, he may still be looking around and tagging cute newcomers with gold stars. He may have written to ten women at the outset, but perhaps, in the month that he's been on the site, he's also added seven new women to his favorites folder. Thus, despite being rejected by seven women initially, the number of members in his favorites folder has remained at a constant thirty.

This, by the way, happens all the time.

Can you now see how it's very possible that a man can find you interesting and attractive, and even list you as a "favorite," and still have never written to you? This is why it's important to initiate contact with other members. If you don't, someone else will. A woman that my friend Dave had listed as a favorite for nearly a year wrote him an email. Even though he was chatting with a few other women at the time, he got back to her instantly and told her that she had long been on his hot list. They've been dating ever since, and I think it's safe to say that they would never have met if she hadn't contacted him first.

News Flash: Men Don't Scare Easily! (At Least the Good Ones Don't)

I can't speak for all men, but we are not freaked out when you write to us. We're flattered! It doesn't happen all that frequently—men still must initiate contact more often—but the balance is shifting. Strangely enough, in my own experience, the people who have contacted me have been far better matches than the people I've contacted. All I know is that I love receiving a letter from a woman who tells me that my profile really spoke to her in some way. In my last year of prolific online dating, the majority of my dates resulted from being contacted, instead of the other way around. This may be an anomaly, but it doesn't have to be. If you're dealing with an evolved and secure man, making initial contact will not make him run for the hills.

If you're a woman without a subscription, it's like standing at the corner of a bar on a Saturday night by yourself, wearing your hottest outfit and waiting for the right guy to come up and hit on you. That's really what you're doing when you're not doing the choosing. The only choices you have are the men who decide to write to you. What about the rest? Well, they may very well have liked your profile, but some swift and savvy women probably snatched them up first.

"Uh, What Is This Charge on My Visa Bill?"

Depending on the site, membership subscriptions can be purchased for one month, two months, three months, six months, or a year. This subscription usually entitles you to unlimited email privileges— meaning you can contact whomever you want, wherever you want, as long as you don't do anything offensive or threatening. Pretty easy if you're not a psycho. Keep in mind that most subscriptions *automatically renew at the end of the billing cycle.* So pay close attention to what you're buying, and read the terms and conditions listed on the website, or you may look at your credit card bill six months down the road and find that you have been charged $24.95 per month for a service that you didn't use beyond the first month. Apart from a few sites like Matchmaker and Dreammates, most established services don't offer any contacts for free, although they will brag about free membership (putting up a profile for no money). The ones that do offer you free contacts are trying to get you hooked so that you will be willing to pay. Most of the sites I'm talking about will automatically renew your subscription at the end of the trial period, whether you like it or not.

Realistically, most people don't find what they're looking for in a month, so the services feel that they're doing you a favor by automatically renewing you instead of sending you a reminder to renew or a cancellation notice. At least that's the party line. The truth is that these companies make a ton of money off of people who don't pay attention when they put their credit card numbers into the computer. It's not a scam, per se—all the terms of the agreement are there on the site—but some people see "one month" or "free membership" and think that it's some sort of trial offer. It's not. Think of it like your cable bill. It will come every single month, even if you never turn on your TV. If you want to cancel your bill, you'd better do it yourself, because the cable company won't do it for you. It will just keep on collecting until you realize you've been paying for a service that you're not even using.

Long-Term Investing vs. Day Trading

Long subscriptions turn out to be good buys for what they give you—the ability to write to countless people for an extended period of time. In late 2003, Yahoo Personals is $19.95 a month, $39.95 for three months, or $89.95 a year, and Yahoo will renew you for the same amount of time and money that you originally purchased. AmericanSingles is slightly pricier but it offers a lower monthly renewal rate. Match.com costs a very reasonable $19.95 a month, $44.95 for three months, or $79.00 a year (with prorated automatic renewals on a monthly basis as low as $6.58 per month). Seven bucks a month! Even as the technology is taking a quantum leap forward, online dating companies are keeping their prices down because they don't want to provide any reason for someone to say no. Take advantage of their generosity and sign up long-term. You won't regret it. Just remember to keep a note on your calendar to cancel before the time's up, or you'll end up paying for the service even after you've fallen in love. Happens all the time.

Not Just a "Token" Mention— Being Selective Saves $$$

Certain websites offer an alternative to the subscription-based service. Tokens (or credits) are individual contact emails or set amounts of one-on-one chat time that you pay for, like putting quarters into a video game. Spring Street Networks uses credits, as do Lavalife, Dreammates, and CupidJunction. For someone like my client Anna, who is very selective in her choice of men and the length of time she takes before meeting them, monthly subscriptions are not the best option. Anna might only write to four people in a month—and if she gets three responses, that's all she needs. If Anna buys, say, 25 tokens for $25 on the Onion Personals, she can make those 25 tokens last for six months because she only uses tokens when she initiates contact. Let me repeat: that's six months for a total of $25, instead of $25 a month for six months, which equals $150. A *big* difference.

For most subscriptions sites, however, I recommend a full year (if, of course, it's affordable). My logic is this: for the frequency with which I fall in love (uh, once, so far) and for the amount of savings that buying a year gets me (I save $200 if I buy a year up front as opposed to paying monthly over the course of a year at $25 per month), it's a no-brainer. The people who have the "I think I'll just try this for a month and see how it goes" attitude are missing the boat. With online dating, you have to make a mental commitment to do it until you have success. Those who quit after a month—whether because they received no response or because they went out with a couple of losers—just aren't thinking ahead.

Why would anyone give up after one bad month? That's like assuming an entire restaurant is terrible because you had one dish you didn't like. In one month, you haven't even begun to scratch the surface of what a website has to offer. Plus, one-month quitters ultimately find themselves right back where they started—single and frustrated—with one fewer outlet to meet new people. Online dating is the best way to meet new people. Less than $40 million was spent on it in 2001; over $400 million is projected for 2003 (Online Publishers Association). Hop on board, y'all.

"Guess What? I'm Going to Drop Fifty Pounds This Month!"

Joining an online dating service is like joining a gym. You don't lose weight simply by signing up. You have to make a concerted effort. If a few weeks go by and you look in the mirror and you don't see any improvement, does that mean you should give up on your workout regimen? No. It just means you have to work harder, use the gym more often, get a personal trainer, and change your workout routine. Same thing here. Putting up a quickie profile, and hoping that your future spouse will sweep you off your feet, is nice, but it's unrealistic. You have to work hard to construct one hell of a personal ad that's going to set you apart, and you have to be active in your search for quality people to contact. As the cliché goes, you get out what you put in. If you want to attain online dating success, you must dedicate yourself to doing it long-term—and hope that you only have to do it short-term.

Cost-Benefit Analysis: A Life Partner for $100

People often hesitate to purchase longer subscriptions not because of the expense but for the following reason: "What happens if I find someone before the subscription is up?" You know what I tell them? "You win." Really, what's the worst thing that can happen? You buy a one-year subscription, you fall in love on the first date, and you're out a hundred bucks. Gee, that's gotta be tough. You just threw that Ben Franklin down the toilet (although you did find a life partner).

If you get hitched within the first few months of getting online, please let me know. You've got Lady Luck on your side and we should probably road-trip to Vegas together. Then you should give your lucky subscription to someone else who needs it. And believe me, you do know someone else who needs it.

For those of you who may be wondering, "What if I buy a six-month subscription [which you shouldn't, given that on most sites you get your second six months for merely $25–$50], I meet someone in the second month, I see him for three months, and then we break up? Can I put my time on hold while I'm in a relationship?" The answer is a big fat no. If Albert Einstein and Stephen Hawking haven't found a way to put time on hold, neither have any of the Internet dating companies.

The only caveat to this "longer is better" rant is if you are unsure of a site's reputation. Your friends haven't referred you to it, you've never heard of it before, and you can't tell how many members are actively using it, but something about the site piques your curiosity. In that case, starting with a one-month plan isn't a bad idea. If the site sucks, you can cancel your subscription before the month is over, and you haven't lost too much time or money.

To minimize your risk, however, the safest bets tend to be the largest, most reputable websites, such as the ones mentioned throughout this book. If you could see into the future, you'd realize that in three months there will be a whole new set of members on the site, any of whom may be "the one." But right now, you can't tell that. And if you quit after only a month, you'll never know what you might be missing.

More Cost-Benefit Analysis— Beer vs. Love

This is no time to be cheap. Even one month, at $24.95, can go a long, long way. That much money can buy you a full month (or six months in Anna's case) of being able to write to a host of interesting people online. Or it can buy you and a date two beers each, plus tip. Which do you think is more cost-efficient? (When in doubt, always rationalize your spending in terms of alcohol.)

Also, guys, consider the actual costs of going on one real date. If you have dinner and drinks for two at a good restaurant, you're not getting out for any less than $75. You know it. I know it. Yet I talk to people all the time who are unwilling to buy a six-month subscription for the same $75. The date is over in a few hours. The website is a long-term investment that can get you date after date after date. So fork up some dough and start writing. This is your love life we're talking about here!

We're not talking about old-school matchmaking businesses like Great Expectations, which will attempt to pair you up with your future spouse for a retainer of a few thousand dollars. No, instead of shelling out all that money up front to let others decide who's right for you, you're taking control of your own destiny. And you're doing it, as Sally Struthers once said, for "less than the price of a cup of coffee per day." With $4 cups of coffee nowadays, we can now claim that the top online dating services cost only 25 percent of a cup of coffee per day. What's worth more to you? The bottom quarter of your vanilla mocha latte or the person with whom you're going to spend the rest of your life?

"HEY, YOU LOOK CUTE. CHECK OUT MY PROFILE."

Writing a Memorable Introductory Letter That Nobody Can Refuse

To harken back to an old simile: your introductory email to a member is like your cover letter to your employer. It's a teaser that lets someone know that you're serious about getting the job. If your cover letter shows that you've researched the company, you like what you see, and you can explain briefly why you'd be a good fit for the job, the HR person will probably go on to read your résumé. If you don't catch the person's attention here, your résumé goes right in the recycling bin.

This Is Your Cover Letter

Bear in mind that people are busy—and we're talking about potential dates now, not employers. So while you don't want to write a generic form letter, you don't want to go too far in the other direction either. Long first letters are even worse than short ones. A woman may check out a man's profile out of curiosity if he writes something brief and boring. She won't, however, contact him after a letter like this:

This Is Your Cover Letter on Drugs

If I did not know otherwise, I might think that you and I are brother and sister. Were I to gaze into my "emotional mirror," I should not be surprised to see you looking back at me. And, throwing aside all modesty, I would list your virtues as my own. I enjoy doing little things that make people smile; what someone once described as "random acts of kindness." I send flowers for no reason other than to bring joy to a friend. I telephone friends and family just to say that I am thinking of them. I am open and honest and not ashamed to candidly share my feelings with my partner. I will support you in all of your endeavors. You will always have a place to rest your head and dry away your tears should life ever treat you unkindly.

I am a lawyer by education and profession; I am anything but a lawyer by temperament and personality. I am an ordinary man with an extraordinary amount and quality of love to share. I have a twinkle in my eyes that shines brightest when reflected in the eyes of someone who has opened her heart to me and shares my happiness. I am easygoing and seldom do I let things bother me. I am naturally gentle and caring. I can be too sensitive for my own good; I put the feelings of others before my own.

My head may be here in the present, but my heart resides in the past. I remember fondly when "mom" was not a phrase. I remember when mom was Mom—not "soccer mom," "tennis mom," or "music lesson mom." I remember how my mom would pick me up when I stumbled, not drop me off somewhere different each day after school. I am blessed that Mom at eighty-four years is still able to look out for "her baby." After living on opposite coasts for more than twenty-one years, Mom recently moved out here to be with her two sons (my brother and me). We have dinner together several times each week. We are each other's best friends. I love her dearly as I know you would after spending just a few moments with her. She would eagerly welcome you into our family.

You are a Viennese waltz among the discord of modern music. You are a field of red poppies. Anyone who earns your love and respect is truly blessed. Let me show you how truly alike we are.

I know that we will be no less than friends.

This email, by the way, was cut by two-thirds. No joke.

It's hard to bad-mouth the passionate and articulate work of a man who is trying so desperately hard to impress this woman, but his words had the complete opposite effect of what he intended. Where he meant to show that he was a nice man with a world of love to give to the right person, what else could a woman think but, "This man needs a life"? He blew any chance he may have had by letting it all hang out in his email. There's wearing your heart on your sleeve, and then there's wearing all of your internal organs on it. Keep this simple axiom in mind for future reference: essays are long, letters are short, and long letters are scary. That's all you need to know.

The question remains, however, if you can't write something short and sweet, and you can't write something long and thoughtful, what can you write? Ah, I'm glad you asked. The answer, not surprisingly, is something in between the two—but closer to the former.

Why Am I Writing to This Person? Now Say It in an Email

Remember, this is your cover letter. Treat it as such. You don't want to start it off with a generic "To Whom It May Concern," but you don't want it to be a two-page tract about how perfect you are for each other, either. My rule of thumb is to step back before writing that opening letter and ask yourself honestly, "Why am I writing to this person?" If you don't know the answer to that question, you might want to save your words for when you're thinking a little more clearly. Because if you can't explain to her why you're contacting her, she won't explain to you why she's not responding to you. Naturally, this kind of advice applies equally to women writing to men. It's just that, like it or not, men still are the ones initiating contact the majority of the time.

Let's say you do know what it is that drew you to her. And let's say, for argument's sake, that it's something other than how attractive she is. If you are going to throw in a compliment about looks—which is fair; people still respond to flattery—make sure that the compliment is specific. "Love your smile," "Great eyes," or "Beautiful hair," is much better than "You're hot." (Not to mention the oft-misspelled variation: "Your hot.")

What will ultimately differentiate you from everyone else who is sending her email is your comment on her profile. Find something that stood out in her essays and give a quick but thoughtful one paragraph response to it. From this, she'll know two things: 1) you've read her essays and 2) you have something in common. Congratulations. You've just leapt ahead of 80 percent of the other emails she's received.

If you're a woman, this is another reason why writing a detailed profile is so very important. Details give your male suitors something to grasp on to when responding to your letter or profile.

Finding an Angle: Easier Said Than Done

Whether you're a man or a woman, if you sound like everyone else, it will be really hard for someone to come up with a way to write to you. How do you initiate conversation with a man when all he writes is that he wants a woman who's "kind, smart, funny, considerate, romantic, sexy, and athletic"? Well, I guess you could say, "Hi. I'm kind, smart, funny, considerate, romantic, sexy, and athletic. I think we'd be a perfect match."

I don't think so.

The goal here is to try and stand out from everyone else in the building, like Allen Iverson during high tea at Buckingham Palace. If I were to respond to a woman's generic profile, I'd have to find a joke, some angle to set me apart. So if she says she's looking for someone kind and smart, I might say something like, "I'm kind of smart. Is that close enough?" The joke obviously doesn't have to be laugh-out-loud funny (nor is it), as much as it has to be an original take on the material you're given to work with. And boy is it easier when someone's giving you more material to work with. Another reason why you should load your profile with specifics—it's much simpler to chat with someone who's given you topics to talk about than it is to strike up email conversation with a stranger with a blank slate for essays.

Examples illustrate the point. Let's say some guy says in his essay that he's a pilot. Maybe you tell him that on your first date he could pick you up in his plane, although it might be tough to find parking on the street. Or maybe she mentions that she likes tropical fish. You could say something about how you do too, especially sautéed with white wine.

Whatever. I know I'm being ridiculous. That's the point. Stand out. Take a chance. If you don't, you risk sounding like everybody else. And in a fast and busy medium like the Internet, sounding like everybody else is about the worst thing you can possibly do. She may look you up if you write something short and sweet, but, then again, if she's really busy, she may not. Therein lies the value of a memorable introductory email.

Surprise! People Love to Talk about Themselves

If your skill set doesn't include the ability to concoct witty and enticing one-liners, you can always try a more conventional route: asking questions. It's a common technique that is effective because it leaves the dialogue open-ended. I rarely use it because I think saying something clever is always better at this stage than saying something earnest. But if you're not feeling clever, there's nothing wrong with closing a letter with a query based on something particular in his/her profile:

"Did you ever go snorkeling in the Caribbean?"

"Can you believe what happened to the Red Sox this year?"

"You must tell me how someone from New York gets into breeding horses."

"Who taught you to bake? Is that a family thing?"

"How long does it take someone to build a birdhouse anyway?"

These questions, while a little forced, at least give the reader something specific to respond to—as if you're having a real-life dialogue, which entails questions and answers and stories. While not ideal, questions are much easier to come up with, and they're definitely superior to the very common form letter, described below.

What Not to Do

- **Give a brief description of yourself, which is already in your questionnaire:** "Hi, I'm Evan. I'm a writer who lives in L.A., and I like sports, movies, and hanging out with my friends and family."

- **Put down your number:** "I'm at 555-323-8611."

- **Ask the person to call you:** "Why don't you give me a call when you get a chance?"

"Why don't you give me a call when you get a chance?" is not an open-ended question. Because the answer is already "no." Leaving your number in your introductory email is the equivalent of saying, "I don't want to put much effort into this letter, but I figure if I write to enough people, maybe someone will respond."

Which reminds me: never give out your phone number in your initial email. That's proprietary information and those are precious digits that need to be worked for. If you're giving them to me that easily, I can only imagine you're giving them to everyone else that easily as well. (I could make an obvious parallel to giving out sex to total strangers, but I won't. Oh. I guess I already did.) The two things to remember here are that 1) no one wants anything that comes too easily and 2) there is no rush whatsoever. I implore you to use every ounce of your power to hold back as much as possible. Resist the temptation to jump into the pool cannonball style, and, instead, try walking down the steps gracefully with your head held high. One is much classier and more appealing than the other. I don't think I have to explain which is which.

A Basic List of Don'ts for Your Introductory Emails

Don't write anything that can be construed as vulgar or offensive, unless that's the nature of the ad or the website. Don't spend too much time describing yourself. Finally, don't write anything that sounds like it could have been written to another person. The first email is meant to interest someone enough into checking you out and writing back to you. It should only be a quick (and highly personalized) paragraph or two. Anything longer than that may veer into "scary, obsessed person" territory, no matter how earnest and sincere your intentions

A Quick-and-Easy Form Letter That Doesn't Sound Like a Form Letter

Behold my quick-and-easy introductory form letter that won't seem like a form letter because you, dear reader, are a creativity machine merely wrapped in human packaging.

1. Start with an eye-catching subject heading—ideally something pertinent to the information in the profile. Let's say she's really articulate and her use of language drew you to her profile. Your header might be: "I'll raise you six dollars for those five-dollar words."

2. Call her by her name, but do it in a playful way. My best friend likes to just use the first initial. If a woman calls herself "Cynthia," he'll start off an email by saying, "Hey C." I like it. I think it's cute and informal, like saying "tu" instead of "usted" in Spanish. Find your own method, but keep in mind that being different is good. Just not weird-different. Weird-different is bad. If you don't know what I'm talking about, ask a close friend of the opposite sex who can be honest with you. Or go back to the section earlier in the book where a very unique woman harbored a very unhealthy crush on a certain actor. That's weird-different.

3. Explain in one paragraph why you're writing to this person instead of everyone else on the website. All people (yes, even men) like to feel special, and even a well-written form letter that has no personal detail will smack of a cold call from a telemarketer at dinnertime. So no more of this "You seem interesting. Check me out and write me back" stuff, which couldn't be more generic. Try something that shows that you read someone's profile and were blown away:

"I must have read a hundred profiles today and out of all of them, you were the only person I felt compelled to respond to. Maybe it was because you mentioned how much you love your dog (I personally can't get enough of my collie), or maybe it was because you said that you like gummy worms (I'm a total sugar addict), but it doesn't really matter. You sound awesome and I just happen to be in the market for an awesome woman."

A paragraph like this is not too long or too sycophantic, but it shows sincerity, warmth, and humor, which are all the elements you need to get someone to go check out your profile online.

4. Close with a confident, warm, and pressureless salutation. Something like: "Write back when you get a chance. Best, Carl." A closing like this shows that Carl is expecting her to respond to him (he's not begging "please write back" or "if you'd like to, write back"); it says that there's no rush to do so ("when you get a chance"); and even if she doesn't return his letter, he wishes her well in the future ("best, Carl"). Simple, gracious, and, therefore, effective.

5. Of course, if you can end on a joke, then end on a joke. Nothing is more attractive via email than a sharp wit.

Writing with Confidence

Below is a letter that a client named Michael wrote to a woman on the Onion Personals who specified that she only wanted to date men over 5'11". Alas, he is only 5'10".

Subject: I thought of being 5'11" just for you . . .

. . . but I figured that if honesty got me this far, why blow it now? I'm 6'1"
in 3" heels and that should be good enough for you to look up into my
eyes when kissing me, dontcha think?

you know where to find me.

M

A little brash maybe, but I thought it was more silly and playful.
At the very least, it's specific and confident.

That last part is key. Be confident. It doesn't matter what gender
you are. People like confident, far more than, say, wishy-washy. What
kind of person would you rather hang out with: a person who comes
off as independent and strong or someone who is so insecure that
they would give their right arm just to be with you before they've even
met you? This may be just my uninformed psychological observation,
but most people don't like it when someone throws himself at them.
We all relish a little chase, a little challenge, a little conquering, and
the gratification of knowing that you reached for and plucked the
highest apple off the tree, instead of the one that was just sitting on
the ground waiting for you to eat.

So aim high. Choose wisely. And take the time to make each person
feel special in your first letter. You'll definitely get a higher response
rate on your initial inquiries than if you cut and paste a form letter to
as many people as possible. Watch, you'll see.

"NO, NO, NO, MAYBE, NO, NO, NO . . ."

CHAPTER 9

Selectively Searching and Choosing Whom to Date

I often tell people: "You can always *not* go out with someone, but you won't have the choice if you don't see them first." When you search on a site, having really stringent search criteria lowers the number of people in your search enormously. I mean, I've heard of people having zero matches on a website because the fantasy person they attempted to find just didn't exist.

There's nothing wrong with knowing what you like. The more experience you have, the more refined your tastes and the fewer people you may be willing to consider. However, if you put in a very narrow set of search criteria, you will be leaving out every person who doesn't exactly meet those criteria. So keep an open mind when searching. It can only help you.

Say that your dream man is 6'0", blue eyes, brown hair, muscular, a nonsmoker, a social drinker, a Presbyterian, and makes over $100,000 a year, and that's what you put into the system. That's great, but just know that if Mr. Right has green eyes, he won't show up in your search. If he lists himself as an "occasional" drinker instead of "social" drinker, he won't appear in your search. In other words, the more specific you get in laying out your criteria, the fewer people you're going to be able to find.

The only things you should specify are the deal breakers. You know what I'm talking about. If you're a woman who is 5'11" and you don't want to date anyone shorter than you, you should include that fact. If you're African American and you want to date only African Americans, specify that. If you are allergic to smoke, it's okay to remove the check mark from the smoker box. But if most of these things aren't a big deal to you, click on "any," or click on every box so that you can be as inclusive as possible.

Expanding Your Search

An apocryphal tale that used to circulate around the MatchNet office is of a man who was searching for a woman thirty-five and younger and a woman who was searching for a man 5'8" and over. A consultant asked the man, "If you met the most amazing woman in the world, but she was thirty-six, would you go out with her?" After a moment, he said he would and then proceeded to expand his search criteria to include thirty-six-year-olds.

Meanwhile, another representative was urging the woman to reconsider her height requirement. As a tall woman, dating shorter men always bothered her, but she realized that, if she had to, she could handle a guy who was 5'7". And she did. If they had kept their searches narrow, the two never would have met. Instead, they ended up getting married. I don't know if I believe the story, but it makes for a happy ending and it illustrates an important point: open up your boundaries as wide as possible. You never know whom you might be missing.

I'd also suggest that you only write to people who you think might potentially be interested in you. This is an easy task because you're told if you qualify right up front in the "Who I'm Looking For" essay. If you choose to ignore this essay, you do so at your own risk. For example, if you're a fifty-seven-year-old woman and a fifty-seven-year-old man specifies that he doesn't want to date anyone over forty-five, you may not want to contact him. He's already told you that he's not interested. Similarly, if a woman writes that she has a predilection for bikers and rockers, you accountants out there should probably save your breath.

Still, despite the bold-faced warning in the profile, people's feelings get hurt when members don't reply. They shouldn't. You wouldn't be insulted if you weren't allowed on a kiddie ride at Disneyland, would you? Then why be bothered if some young woman isn't comfortable dating someone her dad's age? You have every right to contact whomever you want, but you should generally assume that people tend to mean what they say. Don't be shocked if you don't hear back.

I have male friends who will write to a woman regardless of what she says she's looking for, figuring that if just given the chance, they can overcome the barrier in question. I like their optimism, but generally a tall woman who says she doesn't want to date a man who is 5'6" means it. Several angry women have complained about this, and have asked me if there was any way to prevent "disqualified" men from writing to them or from appearing in their search. On most sites, there isn't. But on certain sites you can stop someone undesirable from writing to you multiple times. And on the Spring Street Networks, you can remove members from your search who don't interest you so that you don't have to sift through the same people every time. Companies are starting to give people what they want, but they're not all there yet.

I once had a client named Helen who told me about a man she knew in real life (as opposed to Internet dating life) who was considerably younger than her and was interested in her romantically. Her feelings weren't mutual, but she did manage to check out his online dating profile. There she discovered that she was three years *older* than his desired cutoff age! In other words, he wanted her in real life but never would have looked for her online.

People often don't know what they want until it's right in front of their face. And with Internet dating, you don't have the luxury of seeing that face until you've emailed and talked a few times. After a couple of disappointing dates, many frustrated folks go home, log on to the website, and narrowly restrict their search criteria in an attempt to weed out all the "unwanteds." Suddenly, all they are left with is:

"earns over $100,000," "slim or slender," "master's or doctorate." They think they're raising their standards, when, instead, they're cutting off some amazing people. By acting rash, they don't consider that a wealthy man may check off "none of your business" instead of $100K, or that a slim woman may click on "firm and toned" if she thinks it describes her better. I have no doubt that a great many ships have passed in the night.

Spamming vs. Targeted Marketing

There are two very distinct schools of thought on this matter. The more popular one theorizes that by the very nature of the Internet, as a place where a massive number of people can interact, it's wisest to write to a lot of people. These folks assume, quite correctly, that the majority will either not respond or quickly drop off the radar since they're talking with so many others as well. The theory goes that by building a pipeline of email addresses and phone numbers, you only increase your chances of meeting someone. My best friend likens it to telemarketing. When I disagreed with his approach, he said to me bluntly, "You wouldn't make a living telemarketing to two people, would you?" A fair point indeed.

Nonetheless, I believe it is far better to selectively write to fewer people and have half of them write back than it is to write to hundreds of people and have 10 percent write back. This may be a minority opinion, but that doesn't mean it's the wrong one. The one exception I'd make to my not-so-hard-and-fast rule is if you are intent on only doing this for one month. If you're giving yourself thirty days to fall in love, by all means, paper the town. This chapter is being written under the assumption that you're in this for the long haul and aren't expecting instant gratification.

So why do I advocate a philosophy that's so out of step with almost everyone else out there? Well, let's be logical again. If you have a great profile and the two people you contact respond, you've got plenty to work with. That's what online dating is all about. If those two relationships don't work after a couple of dates, you can always write to two more people and see what happens. If they don't write back, you write to two more. Remember, there's no rush. Just a lot of trial and error.

My best friend is the biggest proponent of the numbers-game theory and it's not my place to tell him he's wrong when it's working well for him. I've even taken the liberty of reprinting his Internet dating philosophy directly from an email he sent me from the next room over.

"I'll usually send out two letters to each of twenty women the first time I sign up. It gives you twice the space in their email box. Write to them fast, because they may not be around for long (and it's nice to get to them before they realize there are creeps on the Internet). Get them while they are still excited about being online. A new caller, so to speak. Also, once they take their pics off, I know I'll never find them again. So, I keep a separate folder of my favorites, so if they do take their picture down, I'm the only one who knows they're attractive. This is a distinct advantage when they are receiving far less email in the future. If I do not get an initial response, I write little teasers every couple of days for a week, and then again every two or three weeks. I just met one woman who didn't respond to me for five emails. Finally she wrote back. She's an unbelievable girl who just got overwhelmed. She even thanked me for writing again."

I love and respect my friend, but I've tried doing this myself, and it just doesn't work for me. But that's why there are thirty-one flavors out there. Everyone has his or her own approach. Then again, you don't need a dating guide to tell you to write to a ton of people. Nearly everyone left to their own devices will start off by writing to more members than they can handle and will set up a series of quick coffee dates. It seems to be a reflex, that feeling that "If I'm paying for this service, I might as well put it to maximum use." Absolutely. If you can keep track of everyone, great. If you can't, just know that there's a working alternative espoused throughout this book.

My best friend's point, however, about many attractive people taking down their pictures quickly, is accurate. If you're shopping for a hottie, you may want to hit 'em quick, or they may be gone the next day. Inbox overflow has already claimed thousands upon thousands of female victims of online dating services.

The perils of mass mailing are manifold. My friend Scott had two women with the same first name leave him messages that said, "Hi, this is Carla. Give me a call when you get in." Melissa kept a list of names and phone numbers by her phone, just in case someone called her unexpectedly. Alex even had a crib sheet with hometown, occupation, and college listings, so he could brush up on details before returning any calls. Personally, I think this is madness, as it's failed me every time.

Why Juggling Is Best Left to Circus Clowns

Consider this: if you juggle two balls at a time, it's not that difficult. But if you try juggling five balls at a time, chances are they're all going to drop. In that case, everybody loses. What happens when you take the mass-mailing approach (which I liken to putting flyers on car windshields to advertise) is that you go through all the people on the website in about a week and leave yourself no one left to write to afterward. All because you thought that Internet dating required writing to large volumes of people. Uh uh. It's quality, not quantity. Quality pictures, quality essays, and quality introductory letters will not only garner a higher response rate than a mass mailer but higher quality members as well.

Internet dating, even done properly, can be overwhelming, especially for women. A woman can put a picture up and have literally hundreds of men writing to her within her first week. That's a double-edged sword if there ever was one. Suddenly a woman who hasn't been meeting enough people has a mountain of men waiting at her doorstep like the paparazzi outside Brad and Jennifer's mansion. It may sound like a problem most people would like to have, but it's not as pleasant as it might seem.

Generally, at the beginning, a woman will look at every man's profile, just to be sure she's not passing up anyone worthwhile. Later, to cut through the "junk mail," she learns to ignore the men who write generic form letters that probably went out to thirty other women that day. Still, an inordinate amount of time is spent sifting through profiles, just to find a handful of men she'd consider meeting.

This is the extreme for women. For men, it works a bit differently.

Men, as in real life, tend to be the aggressors online. In other words, unless you're a really good-looking guy who can sit back and wait for women to write to you, you probably have to make the effort to contact women. As repeated ad nauseum throughout this book, I don't advocate writing to a ton of people at once because it's inherently assuming a lack of success.

The Numbers Game, Broken Down

Consider the possible scenario: You write to a hundred people. All one hundred write back to you. Right. And then you woke up.

Okay, ten write back to you. That's kind of overwhelming. Next thing you know, you're not only taking notes on everyone you're talking with, but each individual becomes less and less important. Inevitably, you lose track of a few of them. Plus, if you're a guy, you may be taking out loans to pay for all of the dates you're setting up.

More realistically, because you put no thought into personalizing your letters, you put up no pictures, and you have short, generic essays, maybe three people will write back to you out of your initial one hundred from the mass mailing. And while you may be satisfied with that, what you've also done is eliminated ninety-seven people whom you can't write to in the future. Damn that numbers game!

If you want to win at this game, you have got to play the numbers better than that.

The mind-set that you should have is not, "If I write to enough people, someone may write back to me," but instead, "If I write to her, she will write back to me." Write to fifty people, get one date, and you have one date. Write to one person, get one date, and you have one date—and forty-nine more people you can write to later if that date doesn't pan out.

Kid in the Candy Store Syndrome

I was amazed when I had men and, occasionally, women calling me to complain when they'd reached the MatchNet "limit" of thirty contacts in twenty-four hours. Invariably they were furious that they were being cut off when they'd paid for the service. I said the same thing to all of them: "Why don't you wait for some of the thirty people to write back before you write any more emails?" Believe it or not, many never considered that. These folks got so caught up into writing to as many people as possible (I call that initial enthusiasm the "kid in the candy store" syndrome) that they never stopped to consider the consequences of doing so—namely that the vast majority would not write back and that, within a week or two, they would exhaust their resources on the website.

That means a paid subscription to a service on which you've now burned through all of your potential leads, and you must now wait for the stock to replenish itself. Lots of people take this approach of signing up, writing to everyone, failing miserably, and then signing up again three months later—only to use the same paper-the-town-with-your-résumé technique. When I admonish clients for using this approach, about half the time, they fervently defend their behavior. Of course, if what they were doing was working, they wouldn't be calling me to begin with, but that's not the point. At this juncture, instead of arguing that my way is better, I usually trot out Ben Franklin's aforementioned definition of insanity and hope that they don't take me too literally.

I am obliged to note that you will never actually use up all of the members of a site. Internet dating is so big that there will continually be more and more people getting online in search of love. This includes first-timers, divorcées, recently broken-up couples, daters who gave up on the Internet before but are coming around again. Keep in mind that if you've written to everyone already, the only people available to you are those who have just gotten on the site and there's stiff competition when writing to new members. Better be prepared to monitor your favorites list and write to people multiple times if you want to get noticed. Personally, that's far too much work for me.

Making the Cut

For just one second, I'm going to get off of my soapbox and look at a hypothetical example in which someone has bothered to take it slowly. Let's say this is a woman who has partially heeded my advice and has written personalized letters to ten people at once. Four write back. Not a bad percentage. Alas, now she's faced with a quandary, as she now has four men to email, to impress, and to keep track of.

Let's add a wrinkle and say that our fictional woman has just had two quality men write to her as well, so now she has six men on her plate. In such an instance, I would highly recommend (and this goes for members of both sexes) saving email correspondence in a folder named after the website you're on. If you're computer-savvy enough, you may even want to create separate folders for each separate person you email. And there will be a lot of people. Most of them will go by the wayside before you ever meet, so make sure you know how to delete folders before you embark on this crazy Internet journey.

That last thought might strike some readers as somewhat of a surprise—"most of them will go by the wayside before you ever meet" doesn't paint a very rosy picture of online dating, does it? Good, because it's rarely, if ever, rosy. Online dating is, at its base, a high-volume medium, which means that if you're emailing six people at once, it's not a bad bet to assume that the six people that you're emailing are also emailing six people at once. Since it's unrealistic to keep that up for very long, we are all forced to make snap judgments based on superficial things in order to thin out the herd.

I wouldn't correspond with any woman who didn't put in the same effort that I put into my emails. If I take the time to write a series of funny and provocative questions, I expect some answers or at least some commentary on what I've said in return. But when all I get is something like, "Cool. What kind of music do you like?" I'm done. You gotta draw the line somewhere, and the lack of thought put into such a response is indicative of one of three things: 1) she's boring, 2) she's not that into me, or 3) she's talking to five other guys. Either way, I don't have the patience to continue to make an effort with a woman who doesn't see the need to make an effort with me; certainly not when there are five other women who are, at least, temporarily interested in me.

This is, admittedly, an extreme stance, developed over four years of online dating experience. And there are plenty of people who don't enjoy the titillating thrill of email the way I do. They would prefer to hop directly to the phone after a very brief exchange. To those people, I would advocate giving people a few emails to prove themselves, rather than cutting them off as quickly as I do. Overall, however, if you write a lot and get little in return, it may just be a glimpse of the relationship to come. And no one wants to be part of a couple where you put in far more than you receive.

"THIS IS HOW WE DO IT."

CHAPTER 10

You Got a Response, Now Don't Screw It Up!

In this chapter, I want to break down many of the variables that you'll be facing when beginning a relationship via email. The rules, for the most part, are no different from the rules that you'd be facing after exchanging numbers at a party—except here you have an edge. You're starting slower, you're getting to know the person, you're feeling him/her out before deciding whether to take it to the next level. If you heed any of what I say, you may not actually meet for a week or two. By the way, this is a good thing.

I'd strongly urge you to store some of this common-sense wisdom for future reference. Like a set of pliers sitting in a box in your basement, you never know when it might be useful.

What Do I Talk About and, More Importantly, Not Talk About?

When you get right down to it, all this online chatter is just like cocktail party conversation. Easy, breezy fun. Again, the advantage is that you already know from his or her profile what this person likes, doesn't like, eats, listens to, and wants in a relationship. That's a huge advantage over making impromptu small talk at a bar. Use this advantage. Read the profile closely. Take the time to construct a personal detailed message—and the second one should be longer than your introductory one. Ideally, at this point, the person who responded to you has asked you questions for you to answer in your email, which makes your job a lot easier. Don't forget while yapping about yourself that the person on the other end wants to talk as well. So after you get done answering her queries, make sure you pose some yourself, so she has something to write back to you.

This is called a dialogue.

If you don't participate properly—if you don't consider where you're leaving off the conversation and how a person could possibly respond to you—you're shooting yourself in the foot. A woman can ask me a dozen questions if she's interested in me, and I can answer them all. But if all I email back to her are my answers, what's she supposed to do now? Ask me a whole new series of questions? Nah. She'll probably focus on a guy who is actually interested in learning more about her, not just in talking about himself. Same as in real life.

I've had more than a handful of people tell me during a consultation, "I don't know what to say to people." In response to that, I can only state the obvious. Be yourself. Talk about you. Ask about the other person. Different individuals are going to have different things to say. It all depends on your life experience. When it comes to topics to discuss, you have no choice but to sink or swim. If you need a list of talking points before you even get together, what are you going to do when you're on the first date? Despite my company name, E-Cyrano, I don't think that email conversations should be carefully scripted. Your profile may be a wonderful advertisement for you, but your conversation *is* you. There's a big difference.

Your saving grace is that everything in life is potential conversation. If you're a decent conversationalist, it doesn't have to come out in the form of a painful Q and A.

"Sooooooo . . . What kind of music do you like? Do you have any siblings? What do you do for a living? How long have you lived here? What's your favorite movie? When was your last relationship?"

Write Like You Talk

These are reasonable questions couched in somewhat stilted phrasing. So instead of approaching your email like you're studying for a test, just write the way you talk. It'll feel natural to you, and others will respond positively to your own comfort level. People who are putting up a front, who are cocky, who try too hard, or who push the envelope with sex talk don't impress at all because their act is transparent. Honesty, depth, and creativity are the keys to these initial email exchanges.

Give longer answers rather than shorter ones because short answers hint that you're too busy for the person on the other end. Keep the conversation light and personal (just like those essays; nothing about your evil ex or your antidepressants, please) and you'll easily be able to differentiate yourself from all the men and women who fail to put in this level of effort.

I've always felt that the best conversations are the ones that flow effortlessly, from tangent to tangent, from story to story, where both parties are engaged, listening and responding. Once again, the fantastic thing about starting with email conversation is that you have all the time in the world to construct your response. This means you never have to say anything lame. Never. Self-censorship is a valuable skill to have because, again, you can't just go around saying everything that you feel. You have to take into consideration the reaction of the person on the receiving end of your "honesty." It's not always going to be pretty.

Flattery Will Get You Only So Far

That's why being able to step out of your shoes into someone else's is an important lesson for this medium. If you don't understand what someone wants, how could you possibly give it to them?

A woman wants to be complimented on her Scrabble-playing ability or on her knowledge of art history or how close she seems to be with her brother. Whatever she wrote in her essay, that's what you should be commenting upon. It's okay to tell someone that you find her attractive, but it's also reasonable to think that she wouldn't want to hear it over and over. Most people don't consider that or, if they do, they don't adhere to it. It's far easier to write, "What's up, sexy? Write me back soon," than it is to compose an original email.

Compliments are fine, but, like everything else, they should be used in moderation. That long introductory letter from Chapter Eight is a classic example of going overboard. Don't forget, you're starting off as perfect strangers, and while it's fun to romanticize and dream that the individual on the other end will fulfill all of your needs, you have no idea until you meet in person. Some people see this as a reason to meet quickly. I still maintain that taking things slowly, weeding people out, and building trust and a friendship beforehand make that first meeting infinitely easier and more comfortable.

Let's Talk About Sex . . . Carefully

Sex is a favorite topic for, well, everyone, but if you're going to go down this road, do it with great caution. And I mean *caution*. Yellow police tape, speed bumps, and orange cones are warning you beforehand, and if you plow through them, you do so at your own risk. You never know how your new online interest is going to react to your proclamation that horses are envious of your equipment. She might think you're hysterically funny for making such a bawdy remark, or, more likely, she might think you're a total pervert for bringing up the subject at all. Some things are better left discovered than stated, and boasts of this nature are at the top of the list.

It's not a contradiction to say that good old-fashioned flirting is not only acceptable but also encouraged during the Internet courting process. After all, when you're trying to charm and romance someone online, the dynamic is definitely different from emailing Grandma. Nevertheless, there's a gray area we tread upon when flirting with someone via email. Not only do you not know what another person's sexual parameters are, you also don't always realize how something that you may consider innocent and flirty may come off as sick and twisted, just because of the nature of the medium. Comedic tone often gets lost in email and, because of that, it's always best to err on the side of caution. For my money, cute double entendres, innuendo, and faux-cocky lines about "when" you end up getting together are a lot safer than coming out and stating your favorite sexual positions. Unless you're on a sex site, in which case . . . well, I don't think I can give advice about how to proceed there.

You should always think, "Could this possibly be taken in the wrong way?" before you write a single word. If it could, don't write it. Or write it, but don't send it. Because the one line that you find sexy and funny may very well be the line that makes her dismiss you and move on to the next person dumb enough to make a comment about her breasts.

Patience Is a Virtue

Presumably you've been single for a while. You're going to continue to be single for a while. Hey, I hope you fall in love tomorrow, but it's not particularly likely. So why act like there's some sort of ticking clock that compels you to have to meet someone right now? Patience is extremely important, and most online daters vastly underrate it. Not just because you're taking your time to get to know someone, but also because patience is surprisingly alluring when playing the dating game.

I'm afraid that, in my experience, human psychology hasn't changed a whit since Internet dating started booming. People still respond to aloofness more than they respond to earnestness. This isn't a ticket to play mind games with the stranger on the other end, and this isn't a plug for the women who wrote *The Rules*. It's more an acknowledgment that if I'm the only guy who writes long, thoughtful emails to a woman, when the rest of the guys are pushing her hard for a date, I'm going to distinguish myself from the pack without even trying.

This is a tactic that is rarely employed but always appreciated. Even if it confuses a woman, it can be effective. Because while other men are throwing themselves at her unsuccessfully, you've managed to keep her interest. By comparison, your laid-back approach seems exceptionally cool and confident. When a woman asks, "Why haven't you asked me out yet?" you know you've done your job. You've reversed the roles. You contacted her, but she's asking you out. All because you didn't press her for an instantaneous meeting, and you remained respectful of her time and space. Being intriguing isn't nearly as tricky as it used to be.

This principle, naturally, applies to women as well. Basic psychology dictates that we want what we can't have, so if you somehow remain unavailable, it's often going to make a man more curious about you. This should not be taken to mean extreme indifference, nor is it carte blanche to be a bitch. Quite the contrary. If someone emails you, respond the next day. If someone calls you, call the next day. Just don't push too hard for a meeting, and you'll find yourself building up trust and interest as time goes by. The longer you wait, the higher your stock rises. To make an analogy, it's not all that different from waiting a few months to sleep with someone. Being unavailable yet accessible is a great technique for both genders.

Don't Act Like It's Christmas Morning

Still, many people, especially first-timers, tend to check their email frequently when they're excited about all the people that they're meeting online. On the other hand, there are folks who are online dating because they're busy doctors or lawyers or factory workers. They don't have time to check their personal email while they're on the clock. Maybe they'll get your note when they get home. Maybe they'll get it the following morning before they go to work. Maybe they'll get it in the morning and won't write back until that night or on the weekend, when they have time to think. It's a refrain I use often in life, and it applies to this situation as well as any: "You don't know what you don't know." You have no idea what's going on in that person's life. Give him/her the benefit of the doubt and allow ample time for a response.

The flip side of this is that most people do check their emails every day. So what do you do if you don't get a letter back in a few days?

Persistence: Dreadfully Annoying or Tactically Brilliant?

My roommate wrote to one woman on Matchmaker eleven times over the course of three months until she wrote back. They ended up dating and remain friends to this day. I lead with this anecdote because it's the exception rather than the rule.

Do not write to anyone eleven times. In all fairness, I will concede that a great deal of my roommate's success has come from follow-up notes. His reasoning, mentioned earlier, is that if a woman is inundated with email from the second she puts her picture up, it might take two or three tries to get noticed. Time has proven him to be correct. As long as you don't sound desperate or angry—"Why didn't you write back to me?!" is no way to begin a charming email—a little persistence can be a good thing. Short letters are fine in this instance. Just make sure you come up with a different angle for each successive letter, so that you will capture the person's attention.

I rarely write to anyone more than once, and if I do, I'll wait a month or two in between letters—hoping that she had someone else in her life at the time, which is the only reason she didn't write back originally.

Generally, however, if someone doesn't write back within a couple days, they're not interested. Hate to say it, but it's true. That person just didn't care to write you back apologetically and wish you the best of luck in your search. This doesn't mean that he or she's a bad person and it doesn't mean that he/she deserves a chastising letter for not returning your email. Try reversing the situation. What if someone wrote to you that you weren't attracted to? Better yet, what if a hundred people contacted you that you weren't interested in? Would you feel the need to write back to each and every one and explain yourself? Most people will take the easy route—ignoring you. It's not right; it's not wrong. It just is. Don't take it personally. Instead, learn to take a hint when someone doesn't write back. It doesn't matter why. Move on.

Maybe she started seeing someone. Maybe he's already talking to three or four women and he doesn't want to complicate things even further. Maybe she hasn't been on the website for six months and just never took down her profile. Maybe you're just not his type. You'll never know, and that's okay. People who pester dating site members into explaining why they were rejected are asking for answers to which they're not entitled. They're begging for answers that they might not want to know. And ultimately, they're driving themselves into a tizzy trying to figure out how someone who seemed perfect on paper could possibly not respond to their ad. Like many things in life, there is often no explanation available.

How and When Do I Take This Out of Cyberspace?

As stated at the beginning of the chapter, I feel that it's best to wait at least a week or two before meeting in person. This isn't as tough as many of your instant-gratification-type friends may make it out to be. All I'm talking about is a few emails, some phone time to see if conversation flows naturally, and maybe a little bit of flirting interspersed throughout this dialogue. I quickly found that if I built a friendship prior to the first meeting, my success rate (getting a second date) sky-rocketed. This more deliberate approach takes confidence (that you won't lose this person to a more aggressive pursuer), as well as time, energy, and, of course, patience. It's not a plan for everyone—especially for those lacking in the above traits.

Naturally, this should be taken on a case-by-case basis, for there is no one way of knowing exactly when to meet someone in person. People looking for hard-and-fast rules, like "you should meet for coffee after three emails" or "you should meet for dinner after five emails and a phone call," are not going to find them here. As long as you exercise judgment in making your decision, there is no right or wrong. Whatever you're comfortable with is the right thing to do.

It's usually men who make "the first move." However, this does not preclude a woman from asking a man out for drinks. Don't be afraid of putting yourself on the line. If you want to meet someone, just say so. Nothing ventured, nothing gained. If the person you ask out balks, you can decide how to proceed next. Guys have to face this all the time. We know it's nothing personal, or you wouldn't be talking to us at all. Most realistically, if someone is taking a long time to ask you out, it's because they're probably seeing a few other people at the same time and are doing their best not to be overwhelmed. Delaying a date is a good strategy, because instead of pressing for a quick meeting, both parties can get a feel for each other in the interim. Dating multiple people may be an example of selective honesty, but if it ultimately helps you get to know and trust someone, it ends up serving a higher purpose.

Things That Should Make You Go Hmmmm . . .

The only thing I'd caution you to beware of is the set of rising expectations that comes with getting to know someone first. Many people—good people, smart people, down-to-earth people—get caught up in the fantasy that they project onto the other person. And once you're in fantasyland, no one can possibly live up to your expectations. Go into a date with cautious optimism. It diffuses the pressure, and you'll have a better time if you don't think of this person as your potential spouse.

Also, don't think that just because you've invested time in getting to know someone that you owe him or her a date. If there's something about him that bothers you on the phone, you may want to keep things on the phone until you decide if it's an issue or not. By the same token, don't let anyone pressure you into a date that you don't want to be on. Neither of you will have fun. There have been numerous times where I've had to talk my roommate out of a date, simply because I can tell that he's not that excited, yet he feels that he should go out with her anyway. The guy probably owes me a thousand dollars based on the number of failed dates from which I have saved him.

Finally, pay attention to consistency. A guy who says that on Friday night he was at the movies with his buddies but tells you on Sunday that he was at a house party is a guy to avoid. Good chemistry is good chemistry, but many people are adept at telling you what you want to hear, in order to get a date. These could be red flags that are spelling out the word *liar*, so watch out for them before you meet in person.

Dumping (or Being Dumped) with Class

Everyone online is forced to make quick decisions based on minor things that we pick up along the way. It's just the way the system works. So when somebody stops corresponding with you (and they will, at some point), don't take it too hard. It's not about you. It's about all the other people out there that are vying for the same person's affections. This is a classic meat market, and there's no point in worrying all that much if some guy likes roast beef when you're the finest smoked turkey around. Know what I mean?

What I urge to everyone when "dumping" someone, whether after an email, a phone call, a date, or a relationship, is to follow the golden rule. If you think it's best to just stop calling someone without an explanation because that's the way you like to be rejected, very well. I can't tell you whether you're right or wrong. I do know, however, that this medium allows people to say things that they'd never say in real life, and they often forget they're talking to a human being. It's much better to make up a white lie like, "I just started seeing someone else and it's starting to get serious, so unfortunately, this isn't the right time for us," than to say, "I can't date someone who doesn't have a job," or "I'm just not that attracted to you." This happens all the time, and you can't take it personally. Rudeness is a statement about the person being rude, not about the recipient of the insult. You're better off without that person in your life anyway.

Anything Else I Should Know?

Of course. Otherwise, there wouldn't be another subheading, now would there? If you're going to invest in online dating—and you've already taken a big step by reading this book—it would serve you well to get to know the ins and outs of the website on which you're posting your profile. The Dating Websites chart that I gave you only scratches the surface and synopsizes what these sites have to offer. Once you find one that appeals to you, take your time to play around with it. Experiment with different search functions, mark off members as favorites, try to send a contact letter (even before paying, though it will probably forward you to a page where you can purchase a sub-scription). The better equipped you are to navigate a site, the more you stand to gain from it and manipulate it to your advantage. I've talked with people who never bothered to make a favorites list because they didn't know how. Which means that each time they logged on, they had to search through all the members to find the one they liked. Talk about a waste of time.

Knowing the nuances of your site will not only save you time and trouble, but it will enhance your entire experience. For example, it's important to find out how the site lists its members in searches. If I'm searching for women, twenty-five to thirty-five, a site may list those women in order of how close they live to my zip code, in order of when they last logged on to the website, or in order of when they last changed their profile. I can choose whichever order I like. Match even lets you search by keyword. For example, if you like the circus, type in "circus," and anyone within your parameters that also wrote circus will come up in a search. Friendster is based on this principle as well. Matchmaker allows you to search for compatible singles down to the smallest details: hair color, astrological sign, or type of job. If you know you only want to date a red-headed Aries veterinarian, you've come to the right place.

Knowing how to navigate a website's search function can directly impact the number of contacts you make. Say you wrote an amazing profile, but you haven't changed it in a year. And say the site lists people in order of how recently profiles are changed (this is to keep the "new blood" at the top of the list). What this means is that anyone who created a profile after you has cut in line ahead of you. That's thousands of people, which means that, in all probability, nobody has seen your fabulous essays for months.

Every dating site has a "help" section, which answers these kinds of questions, plus a whole bunch that you wouldn't even think to ask. Sometimes there are functions on a site that aren't obvious at first glance—such as a contact log—which can be very useful once you start corresponding with multiple people at once. So look around. Play. Explore. You may be delighted at what you find.

TEN WAYS YOU KNOW YOU'RE
HOOKED ON INTERNET DATING

1. You stay logged on the website even after you go to sleep, to stay visible and make people think you're still online.

2. You have more email addresses, passwords, and usernames than you have fingers and toes.

3. You have email folders specifically for your online dating friends.

4. You start seeing the same people's profiles on multiple sites. And you can't make fun of them because you're on those sites too.

5. You get renewal charges on your credit card bill from sites you didn't know you signed up for.

6. You turn down the volume on your answering machine before a date, just in case another Internet person calls while your date ends up spending the night.

7. You spend less time at work than you spend searching, emailing, and calling dates from home.

8. You keep a crib sheet by your phone to keep track of all of your dating prospects, their occupations, colleges, hair colors, and hometowns.

9. You check for a message from one person while driving to go on a date with another person.

10. You have no idea whom to call back when the voice on the answering machine says, "Hi, it's me."

"LET'S *NOT* MEET FOR COFFEE."

CHAPTER 11

How Caffeine Kills Chemistry and Other Controversial Theories on Dating and Dating Safety

Please take whatever I say in this chapter with a grain of salt (or whatever condiment works for you). I'm going to espouse some dating theories that run counter to what a lot of so-called experts suggest. I offer these ideas not to invalidate their ideas completely but rather to suggest an alternative that I have found to be more effective.

I'd like to begin by debunking the school of thought that says that you should meet a member ASAP. The reasoning behind meeting quickly is to see if you have chemistry right away before you invest any time in the "relationship." Now no one can deny the importance of physical attraction. But consider this: you are far more likely to have a disastrous first date if you rush into it without getting to know the other person beforehand. Agreed? So, as advocated often throughout this book, slow down. Email for a while. Flirt a little bit. Exchange numbers. Talk on the phone a few times. At this point, you can actually weed out people who aren't right for you—all before you even go out on your first date. To me, this is not time wasted. This is time saved. A few emails and a few phone conversations will take a shorter amount of time and cost infinitely less than a bad date.

The Author's Detractors Speak!

A woman I once dated told me that she wholeheartedly disagreed with my approach. Here is the email she wrote me, explaining why: "I don't want a pen pal and I'd rather meet someone sooner rather than later. You can say that the time spent getting to know each other isn't wasted . . . but honestly, in today's fast-moving world, I think it is time wasted. I personally don't want to spend a month writing and chatting with someone, then meet them in person and find out there's no romantic clicking at all."

Fair enough, but my quick rebuttal would be to say that two days of email and five days of talking on the phone aren't an incredible investment of time. Plus, it can go a long way in terms of building up trust prior to that first date. Just something to think about while you're being bombarded with requests for coffee by complete strangers.

Naysayers will claim that, in the end, it's all about chemistry. I won't deny that. The school of thought for most online daters is that, if you can meet quickly and determine chemistry, you don't have to spend potentially two weeks getting to know someone on the phone, only to find out that there's no "click" in person.

Said Amy, a friend from grad school whom I had previously consulted with at MatchNet, "Several times I had intriguing emails, delightful phone conversations, and was really looking forward to meeting the guy. Could hardly wait. Until I saw him, and in four seconds I knew there was no way. Not just physical attractiveness, but chemistry. It's either there or it's not. All that time, all that anticipation, and for what?"

Well, for starters, getting to know someone for a few weeks prior to the first date builds up a sense of anticipation and excitement. What sounds more appealing to you—a first date over dinner or drinks with a person whom you know and like? Or a quick coffee date with a total stranger to find out if there's chemistry? I can virtually guarantee that if you take your time before meeting someone, you won't have a bad date and, even if there's no love connection, you'll likely walk out of that evening with a brand-new friend. Those friends may not only turn out to be valuable in your life, but they may turn out to have friends of their own. Don't discount the importance of friends of friends. They can be like a dating site unto themselves.

Must I Tell You What to Do When Life Gives You Lemons?

In one instance, my client Kenneth was passed along after a date from one woman to her best friend, who she thought was a better fit for him. Believe it or not, after going out with that second woman, Kenneth was actually recommended to *another* friend of hers. Many men would find this embarrassing (Kenneth did too), but the silver lining is that it was sort of flattering. It wasn't that these women didn't like him. Evidently they thought highly enough of him to hook him up with their own close friends. It didn't work out, but who knows? It could have. At least he was out there meeting people, even if he was being passed around like a joint at a fraternity party.

I also have a feeling that part of the reason that those follow-up dates didn't work well was due to the fact that Kenneth didn't take the time to get to know any of these women before he met them. Essentially, he was being set up on a bunch of blind dates and, as many of you know, there are few things more inherently awkward than blind dates.

Unfortunately, for many people (that is, those who are not reading this book), online dating becomes nothing more than a dizzying series of blind dates. The reasons are clear: "Hey, we're all busy adults with careers and friends and responsibilities. Who has time to waste with people who are probably not right for you anyway?" So, two emails and a ten-minute phone conversation later, you end up meeting a complete stranger for a cup of coffee. Regardless of whether you saw a picture beforehand, you're still talking about a blind date here.

And what are blind dates, really, but informal interviews? Unnatural, weird, we-know-nothing-about-each-other-type interviews. It is possible to make a great connection with a total stranger over coffee.

It's also possible that I'll be struck by lightning while typing this. There's a reason that they say that the best relationships are forged from friendships—and if you're trying to start a relationship with a brief meeting over a latte, I strongly feel that you're handicapping that relationship's chances from the get-go.

When I first started Internet dating, I did all the things I've cautioned against: writing impersonal letters to dozens of women, taking more phone numbers than a bathroom wall, and penciling in half-hour coffee dates three or four nights a week. It's not a coincidence that none of those women stayed in my life for more than a third date.

Noted dating expert, psychologist, and author Eve Hogan came to my former company one afternoon to give a five-hour seminar on the art of online dating. Eve is a fabulous speaker who really knows her stuff. Toward the end of her session with us, she brought up a series of basic rules that she felt people should follow when meeting for the first time. The rules are exactly what you'd expect—you can probably find them in any online dating book—and all are designed with a woman's safety in mind.

> *"Don't let him pick you up at your house."*
>
> *"Arrive separately and meet for a quick cup of coffee at a public place."*
>
> *"Make sure the date takes place during the daytime."*
>
> *"Tell your friends where you're going."*
>
> *"Plan an escape—either a friend calling on your cell phone after an hour or a 'meeting' you have to attend later in the day—just in case you get trapped on a bad date."*
>
> *"Insist on splitting the check, so he doesn't feel like you owe him anything."*

These are all reasonable points—in fact, I'll go so far as to say they're smart points—things which I'd be remiss not to mention in this chapter.

Is There Such a Thing As Overly Cautious?

Still, the overriding tone of Hogan's pointers is a certain wariness and an overall sense of distrust. These safety rules all assume the worst from your date, instead of the best. And while it's not bad life advice to expect the worst and hope for the best, so that you're never disappointed, I don't think that's the greatest way to go into a date. Positive, upbeat, and confident always beat wary, mistrustful, and jaded. Again, how you initially meet someone has a lot to do with how you'll interact thereafter. Approaching someone at a bar is different from being introduced to that same person by a friend at a party. One is much more comfortable than the other, so while it may be the same people meeting, the results will likely be quite different.

What could be worse than a date where you're coming in with your guard up and all systems on DEFCON 4? Don't get me wrong, I would never dismiss the safety factors that a woman has to consider, and lord knows, I've heard enough dating horror stories about overly persistent men to last me a lifetime, but this book isn't being written for the stalkers of the world. If you're a stalker, please put down this book. Really. I don't want your business. You give the rest of us guys a bad name, and you make it infinitely harder to get women to trust us.

Maybe I'm a naive idealist, but I happen to believe that people are good at heart. It's not a stretch to say that most people are out there in search of that elusive thing called love. And love doesn't come easily. You have to go through a lot of people in order to find it, but it's definitely worth the effort once you have.

Showdown at the MatchNet Corral

Anyway, when Eve Hogan got to the part about the man letting the woman split the coffee tab, I just couldn't help myself. I raised my hand high in the air like Arnold Horshack, just begging to be called upon by Mr. Kotter.

"Yes?" Eve said kindly.

"Yes, hi. My name's Evan and I've done a lot of Internet dating myself. While I totally agree with almost everything you said so far, there are two things that I strongly differ with you on."

"Really, what are they?"

"Okay, for starters, you should just know, right off the bat, that caffeine kills a date. Apart from scaling fish or sifting through trash for aluminum cans, sipping coffee by daylight is about the least romantic thing you can possibly do. Secondly, if a guy lets a woman split the check with him on the first date, there's *no way* he's getting a second date."

Everyone laughed, including Eve. This gave me the courage to continue. Not that I'm all that shy to begin with.

"Personally, I think the best way to meet someone is to wait until you've been talking for a while and you've built up a level of trust. By this point, she knows that you're not a psycho-killer, and are, for the most part, a nice guy. So when you tell her you want to take her out for drinks instead of trying to jam coffee into your busy weekend schedules, she'll be excited because it's a great departure from her standard coffee/interview date."

More laughter. Some nodding heads. I was on a roll. And nobody was stopping me. I couldn't believe it.

"Furthermore, going on a 'real date' changes the mood entirely, injecting romance and excitement into the equation. On a 'real date,' I can pick you up at your home, escort you to my car, open the door for you, and take you out to a dark bar for a few rounds of drinks that I'm going to pay for myself. The nighttime setting sets the scene for us to dress up a little bit, while the mood and the alcohol accomplish one very important goal."

"What?"

"I know I look a lot better when it's dark and my date is a little drunk, and I'll bet she probably looks better too."

Once again, everyone laughed. I wasn't kidding, though. Think about it. Instead of plastic chairs outside a crowded Starbucks at 3 P.M., we now have a different arena, where both parties are dressed to kill, eager to meet, and slightly tipsy. Therefore, the whole tone of the conversation has changed from stilted and formal to loose and fun. Like it or not, liquor is a great social lubricant in the way it lowers your inhibitions. And, to be honest, it's why my dates went much better after I decided they'd take place in dark bars.

Post-Modern Feminist Deconstruction Theory: Who Pays?

I've talked about online dating being an excellent means to break free of the customary gender roles that bind us. This is most evident in the success that women have when writing to men online. However, there is a bastion of tradition that has been left intact, despite the many changes in society. This is the time-honored practice of men paying for women.

Let me be clear. I pay for the first date and the second date unquestionably. Do I think it's fair, given that everyone I go out with makes more money than I do? Of course not. Life isn't fair. For whatever reason, the same standards of equality that have allowed more women to graduate from college than men in 2003 haven't caught up to the dating world. I wish it weren't that way, but it is. If you're a man, you risk not getting a second date if you allow your date to pick up the check. This has been confirmed to me by countless women. Generosity is an important trait, and therefore, there's no value in quibbling over a few (or more than a few) dollars if it means that you won't get a second date because you're perceived as cheap. Suck it up and put it on credit, my friend.

Naturally, there are other takes on this matter. One says that whoever made first contact should pick up the tab. Another says that the parties on a first date should always go dutch and split the check. Still another, proposed to me by a woman, suggests that it would be a nice gesture for the woman to foot the first bill.

Here's God's honest truth: men have no idea what to do. We'll do whatever you want. Anything that lets you know that we respect you and allows us to see you again. The thing is: we can't know how to play it unless you are really direct about it over the phone. For example, you saying, "I *always* insist on splitting the check on a first date," gives us a pretty solid idea about what to expect. At least then we know that when you're doing the "reach," you actually mean it. More often, when a woman reaches for the check, men have been conditioned to say, "No, no, no. I got it. I insist." That's cool. Hey, it's tradition. But tradition doesn't take into account the nuances of modern dating where a woman often makes more than a man.

If you're looking for definitive answers, you won't find them here. Based on my personal experience, one thing I can say to men is this: if you insist on paying, and she insists on splitting the check, you might as well let her do it. Don't bother saying, "Fine, but I've got the next one." The truth is, she's not interested in you and is trying to show it by not allowing you to pay for her. Might as well save yourself a few bucks since you're never going to see her again.

Breaking the Male Code for the Sake of Female Safety

I need to say one final thing—and I didn't realize this was such a mystery until a friend from MatchNet pointed it out—and that is, one of the reasons why a man may want to pick up a woman at her home for a date. I thought it was obvious, but my friend, who is an attractive woman and a frequent dater, had no idea just how simple and direct the male mind can be.

Anyway, apart from basic courtliness and chivalry, both of which have a good amount of value on a first date, the main reason that men insist on driving is because it gives them the best chance of coming home with a woman at the end of the evening. I never found this sneaky, because I thought that it was just an unspoken but obvious truth. However, further research has shown that this is a shocking revelation to some women. It shouldn't be.

If Harry meets Sally for coffee, what are the odds that he's going to land in her bed afterward? If you answered, "No shot in hell," you'd be correct. If Harry and Sally drive separately to a local pub, tie on a few brewskis, and find themselves really attracted to each other, what is the likelihood that he's going to be buying her break-fast the next morning? Zilch. Sally may give Harry the good-night kiss, but they're not driving separate cars back to her place. The momentum is killed the moment they enter their own vehicles. This means that the only way for Harry to get Sally to fake an orgasm for him is to pick her up in his '97 Honda Accord and hope that charm, chemistry, alcohol, and the necessity of her getting home may result in an invitation upstairs.

Ladies, I'm sorry to break this news to you.

Fellas, I'm sorry that I broke the code, but women deserve to know what they're in for. Safety counts for a lot when your date out-weighs you by fifty pounds or so.

I do not adhere to the sexual double standards that say that "he's a stud" and "she's a slut." First date, tenth date, it makes no difference to me. But if you want the option of making a date last longer than dinner or drinks, take the same transportation. If you believe that taking your time is better for the sake of the relationship (if not the libido), then meeting out should be your plan.

Needless to say, not everyone wants to lose their inhibitions on a date, and not everyone wants to spend $50 on drinks for a stranger. Some folks don't even drink. Plus, there is a certain illusion in going out for a romantic evening, where the mood might make you think there's chemistry in the air when there really isn't anything in the air except for the smell of scotch. So there are a variety of reasons why going for drinks wouldn't be right for everyone. The moral of the story isn't that drinking booze means a good time for all. The salient point is that absolutely anything, to me, beats a stagnant, unnatural, half-hour coffee interview.

Only one coffee date ever worked for me, and it was with a woman who happened to live on my block. We had a pleasant enough time when we went out (in this instance, it was for fruit smoothies, not coffee), but there was no "spark." Then again, it is hard to manu-facture chemistry over any drink where a straw is involved (Mai Tais in the Caribbean excluded). To this day, this woman remains my best female friend, and, from time to time, I can't help but wonder: what if

I had met her under different circumstances? Say, at a dark bar over a couple of vodka martinis.

The word of mouth I've gotten from female clients and friends is that it's better to be safe than sorry. I'd like to tell you to simply trust in the goodness of mankind, but I will concede that I'm coming from the male perspective. In other words, I've never personally been concerned for my safety when giving out my phone number or when inviting a woman into my apartment. I believe that most men are nice guys, but, in the event that five percent are not, it's probably wisest to err on the side of caution and meet at a public location. Yes, I'm contradicting my own advice. Or at least modifying it.

I'm still going to insist on drinks over coffee though.

A Plan B for Teetotalers

Listen, if the bar thing doesn't work for you, you can always get creative. Do something fun in the daytime where you're not forced to look each other in the eye for two straight hours. Go rollerblading. Go window-shopping. Go bowling. Go hiking. Action-plus-talk is far easier than just talk. When you're doing something, you're not forced to carry on consistent conversation for the entire first date. You also have the stimulus of the activity to comment upon as well. Personally, I find that nothing bonds two total strangers quite like making fun of other total strangers. But that's just me. Don't book an entire day, because, on the off chance that you're on a bad date, you should have the ability to call it quits after a few hours.

Bear in mind that all of this advice—this entire book, really—is dependent on both participants being morally decent people. The Internet, unfortunately, can't police its own inhabitants. That's your job, and another reason to (have I said this before?) take your time before meeting someone. The sad truth is, bad people are going to be found everywhere. At work, at the laundromat, next door, and, yes, on the Internet, too. So while I am being somewhat glib about safety issues, I would never suggest that any woman flippantly ignore all of the aforementioned precautionary measures.

I met my last girlfriend after two weeks of frequent and lengthy emails and a few three-hour phone conversations. In this rare instance, she picked me up at my place, whereupon I paid for our sushi dinner. Apparently she trusted me (I assume it was due to our interaction prior to the date), and we ended up back at her place that night. Please don't tell her parents.

Since I can't vouch for any other guys, my advice to women would be that playing it safe is never a bad idea. I would add, however, that if a woman has taken the proper time to get to know someone via email and phone, she should be able to trust her gut about whether or not to let a man pick her up at her home. The advantage of driving together is that you will end up on a more traditional date, and there's the opportunity for some post-date extracurricular activity. If this doesn't interest you, or if you don't feel you can trust yourself because your instincts have been wrong before, then, by all means, follow those aforementioned safety rules.

And please tell your friend who will "accidentally" call you at the coffee shop an hour into the date that I send my regards.

"IT ALL SOUNDS SO GREAT. WHAT COULD POSSIBLY GO WRONG?"

CHAPTER 12

Stalkers, Scams, and Chat Rooms, Oh My!

The Internet is akin to the Wild West of the late 1800s. There's a whole bunch of people out there, but it's still largely a free-for-all, a vast lawless frontier where people can get away with anything with near impunity. The anonymity of the computer creates a barrier— somewhat like a Plexiglas wall—that gives people the impression that they're actually getting close with someone when, truly, all they're doing is pressing their nose up against the glass. This isn't to say that people can't get close online. They can, and they do all the time. I've heard the most heartwarming stories of people falling in love before they even met in person and then living happily ever after. A seventy-two-year-old woman from Pittsburgh told me that a seventy-eight-year-old man from Kansas was going to move out to marry her, so they could live out the rest of their golden years together. A very close friend of mine just got married to someone he met online. A woman I dated is living with the guy she met online after me. Obviously, somebody's getting lucky on the Internet, or there wouldn't be this proliferation of positive anecdotal evidence.

Unfortunately, the seedy underbelly of online dating, the dark lining to the silver cloud that I've been extolling throughout this entire book, is still very much in existence. Bad people do bad things online that they couldn't get away with in real life, and there's pretty much nothing you can do about it. All you can do is be aware, be cautious, and think before you act.

Scams are perpetrated on dating sites all the time. Most of the time it's relatively innocuous—a woman's profile is occasionally a front for a pornographic website. Some women online are actually prostitutes who find this to be a much cheaper and safer way of looking for clients than walking the streets. There are some women online from other countries—Russia immediately leaps to mind—who are part of a mail-order bride racket. There was a case in the news in 2003 about a military man who was serving overseas and dating online. It was discovered that he had proposed to fifty women all over America. They were all suing him, although I'm not sure there's a statute against being a dick.

The worst offense I heard personally was from an older man who called my former company to complain that he had been corresponding with a woman from Russia who had scammed him out of two thousand dollars. It seems that he had written to her and she professed to be very interested in him. She played him like a fiddle—sending frequent emails and pictures over the course of a few months. Finally, she decided it was time to fly out to meet her online American lover. Sadly, she didn't have the savings to afford the round-the-world trip. The guileless man did, though, and he sent her enough money to not only fly to America but to move all of her stuff with her so that they could be married. The check went to a post-office box in St. Petersburg, and the man never heard from the woman again.

He was understandably furious, but all we could do was to cancel the woman's account, which meant nothing because she could sign up again under another fake email address. Since she never paid by credit card, there was absolutely no way to trace her whereabouts. The poor guy was, in a word, screwed, and all because he was the kind of person who would never even consider the idea that he might be the victim of a scam. Honest people don't have criminal minds and are therefore more prone to being scammed because of their naïveté. So don't be naive. People lie. I can't tell you who they are, but I can say this: if it sounds too good to be true, it probably is.

"Hello, Is Anybody There? Hello?"

Almost all websites offer to let you browse their members before signing up. This is a good thing, but be careful. Just because you see an attractive person on the site doesn't mean he/she's that attractive in real life, and it doesn't mean he/she's frequenting the website anymore. It's entirely possible that if you write to her, you might be catching her a husband and two children later. Seriously. Lots of people sign up for multiple dating websites, fall in love, and simply forget to remove their profiles. On certain sites, where it doesn't say the last time a person logged in, you really can't tell if a person signed up five years ago or just yesterday. Also, make sure there are enough active members in your area before paying for services. A site may claim forty thousand members in South Carolina, but if only a hundred are within a fifty-mile radius of you, you're as screwed as the guy with the Russian girlfriend.

Stalkers Be Gone!

The most common stories I hear as a consultant have to do with online daters' inability to deal with rejection. It's understandable— rejection brings out the worst in people. It opens old wounds and reveals the raw insecurities that we have heretofore managed to keep covered. If you're not confident about your looks, the time after a rejection is when you'll dwell on your looks. If you're not confident in your intelligence, you may very well find yourself up at night wondering if you're smart enough. Being hurt, being sad, being angry, being confused, this is all normal human behavior.

What is *not* normal is calling someone on the phone at 3 A.M. to demand an answer as to why she's not interested in you. Not normal is writing threatening and insulting emails to a person who has done nothing wrong except tell the truth. Showing up at someone's office unannounced, when he never even told you where he worked? Not normal. Anything more than a classy parting phone call or email, saying that you're disappointed but that you wish him/her the best of luck, is not normal.

Rejection occurs in virtually every relationship that you'll ever have. One person or the other will eventually decide that things just aren't working out and that you'd be better off apart. The rejected can question and question and question, but the bottom line remains the same: it's time to move on. And I think we can all agree that an elegant exit from the stage is far more appealing than being dragged out kicking and screaming by the bouncers.

Getting blown off is tough, but you must realize that there is nothing to gain by holding on to a relationship that someone else has already let go of. I'm not just talking about the loss of pride that a person inevitably suffers by becoming a certifiable loony but also the ripple effect of such behavior on everyone around you.

Yes, stalkers, I'm talking to you! (Non-stalkers, you can just skim this part.)

Tell me: If you love her so very much, why are you going to such lengths to make her miserable with the prank phone calls? If you cared about her yesterday, when you were still dating, how did she suddenly become a bitch overnight? Turning the tables, let's say you broke up with a woman after a few dates, a few weeks, or a few months, would you want her to make your life miserable the way you're doing it to her right now? No? Then get a grip, champ. There are plenty of other women available, and, no matter how bruised your ego, if you can't get past this in a timely fashion, everybody loses. I had to suspend more accounts in my time at MatchNet than I'd care to admit due to such devoted rejectees, most of whom developed their attachments after only one date or sometimes after just a few phone conversations. These people are no reason to shy away from Internet dating—you could just as easily meet a freak at a mutual friend's cocktail party—but they are a perfect example of why you should be selective before going out with someone for the first time. And, for the record, women do stalk men as well. It's just not as prevalent, nor as dangerous, so there's nothing on which to elaborate. But, lest you think I'm picking on guys, psycho behavior isn't unknown to the fairer sex as well.

Getting Your Stalker to Stalk Off

If you find that someone you're dating, talking to on the phone, or just emailing can't take a verbal hint, stop all correspondence immediately. You will never get the last word with your stalker. Every email or phone call that you make in attempts to sever ties is seen as an invitation to continue stalking. To choose an unpleasant analogy, it's like passing by a panhandler on the street. Once you've made eye contact with the panhandler, you've essentially extended an invitation for him to ask you for money. If you ignore him, perhaps he won't ask, and you can proceed to your destination. Ignore your stalker.

If you have evidence of a person writing lewd or threatening emails, be sure to save them in an email folder and forward them to the online dating company where you met. Although the company is not liable for anything that happens in the real world, most companies will suspend the stalker's account to prevent further harassment. Unfortunately, this is only a temporary solution, as any moderately savvy person can get back on the website by filling out a new account using a different email address. If this happens, and the stalking continues, you may want to "block" the person from contacting you on the website, avoid the chat rooms, hide your profile, and decline any new email that seems suspicious. Alerting your local authorities is not out of the question, as long as you have saved the emails that indicate a threatening pattern of behavior.

For Those Who Miss the Stimulating Conversation of the Algonquin Roundtable: Chat Rooms

Another frequent source of Internet dating frustration is the chat rooms that are quite popular on these sites. The one great thing you get in a chat room is live conversation, which is superior to email any day. The kind of conversation you'll get in a chat room, on the other hand, leaves much to be desired. The "anything goes" atmosphere plays like a loud fraternity party. Fraternity parties were great . . . when you were nineteen. Now picture forty people acting like horny teenagers, talking over each other in online shorthand, and you'll get a good idea what chat rooms are all about.

I'm 30/m/LA. Any ladies in the house?

Hey, NY!

U look hot, Gina. Got more pix?

Anyone wanna chat privately?

I think that if Shakespeare were alive, he would have written for Buffy.

ROFLMAO!!

Nancy!

Poloman!

Wazzup, NY?

24/f/Boston. Looking for cute boys.

Anyone wanna chat privately?

Goddamn Giants cost me $100.

What's your email, Terminator?

Sux for u. : (

I'm a cute boy!!

I'll suck for you, Polo. LOL.

Phone call. Brb.

Hi, BigHeadTodd.

Ignore him. I'm cuter. ;-)

G'night, everybody!

Seriously, Joss Whedon is just as talented as the Bard.

I'm never betting again. No f-in way.

G'night, Hunneybear.

SexxxxxyLexxxxy. Check out my URL.

Anyone wanna chat privately?

Not to generalize, but that's essentially the transcript from any chat room, on any website, at any time. Except in real life, the spelling is much, much worse. It's a train wreck. It's a car chase. It's Jerry Springer. It explains why we're in the bottom quartile in education among Western industrialized nations. In short, this author finds chat rooms appalling. But, hey, lots of people love them just like they love professional wrestling. It's your call.

The positive side is that chat rooms are fast and usually free. Could there be a more predictable indictment of what's wrong with online dating (and the world) than something that is immensely popular because it's fast and free? Especially since all I've been saying for two hundred pages is that you should pay for a service and take it slow?

By all means, do as you please, but also recognize that people are much ruder in chat rooms than they are anywhere else. The simple reason why: because they can be. No one can stop them. No one can yell at them. All people can do is ignore them, which isn't much solace if some jerk starts calling you names for no apparent reason while you're trying to have a pleasant conversation with someone else. No, chat rooms aren't a scam. I just don't think that they lend themselves to good one-on-one conversation, which, to me, is the foundation of any nascent relationship. Stick to writing short, funny, personal introductory emails to a handful of people, and you'll be much better off than trying to get a word in edgewise over a guy named SpazTick who can't tell the difference between "there," "they're," and "their."

" . . . AND THEN, AFTER I GOT MY M.B.A. FROM HARVARD, I WAS NAMED VICE PRESIDENT OF OPERATIONS AT A DOTCOM, BROKE UP WITH MY GIRLFRIEND OF THREE YEARS, AND MOVED OUT WEST TO BECOME A SCREENWRITER."

CHAPTER 13

Knowing When to Shut Up and Listen (and Some Other Dating Tips You Might Find Useful)

There are entire books about the art of dating, and I'm not going to attempt to cram one of those books into a short chapter. I will say, however, that there are some things to keep in mind when going on a date that are relatively universal. One of the biggest traps, as alluded to in the chapter title, is talking about yourself too much. I am, I regret to say, a multiple offender, but I've learned my lesson. These days, if I want to talk about myself, I write a book; on dates, I try to ask a whole lot of questions.

Your date, you may be surprised to know, doesn't necessarily want to get a verbal dissertation about why you're the perfect person, much less the perfect person for her. Instead, all she desires is flowing conversation. Below, a simple example of a flowing conversation:

Person A asks a question. Person B answers that question and tells a pertinent story. Person A asks a question relevant to that story. Person B answers that question, and poses a new question to Person A, who breaks out with a story that leads to more questions.

See how this works?

This shouldn't take a diagram, but many people lose the ability to reflect upon their own behavior when on a date. Witness shows like

Blind Date, in which people do the stupidest things and don't even realize it until they see the videotape, when it's way too late to recover from their mistakes. You will not have a videotape to record your mistakes, so you have to try a little bit harder not to make them. Once in a while, if you notice that you've been dominating the conversation the way the Yankees dominate the Tigers, you might just want to stop and apologize for yapping so much.

Copping to a flaw is much better than being unaware of it—and if you can catch yourself in midstream, after going on for fifteen minutes about yourself—you may even be forgiven for it. Better yet, she may even tell you that she finds your stories interesting or funny and give you free license to continue your monologue. Still, most people would rather talk about what they know best (themselves) than listen to some stranger prattle on about the time he saved a spotted owl while working with Habitat for Humanity in Portland. Although I'm sure it's a really good story.

TMI (Too Much Information)

Another thing that trips up a lot of people is what is commonly known as TMI, or Too Much Information. Yes, believe it or not, baring your soul on a first date is almost universally considered a dating no-no. There is a time and place for everything, and the time for psychotherapy is from 1 to 1:50 P.M. on Tuesdays, not from 10 P.M. to 2 A.M. on Saturday nights. We all have our vulnerabilities, our anxieties, our fears, our baggage, our hang-ups, our insecurities, and our skeletons. Leave them at home, the same way you do when you go to work each morning.

Just because you have a rapt audience for a few hours doesn't mean that you need to air all of your dirty laundry in that time. I can only say this stuff because I have, at times, been guilty of this myself, and I certainly sabotaged some decent dates with my inability to shut my mouth. (I can only imagine a handful of women I've gone out with nodding their heads right now in unison. A blanket apology to all of you.) Some of us have to learn the hard way. Others can read books instead.

Here are some other little things that I think are important to remember.

Basic On-Date Etiquette

Make eye contact. Not staring. Just eye contact that shows that you're paying full attention to the person in front of you. Looking down at your food shows a lack of confidence. Looking past a person's head at the passersby indicates a lack of interest.

Turn off your cell phone. Unless you're a doctor who's on call, there's really no excuse for being interrupted when your attentions should be focused on your date. When there are stories being told, ask questions. When there are topics being discussed, offer opinions. There is nothing more boring than someone agreeing with everything you say. Disagreement is healthy and interesting, but only if both of you can agree to disagree without letting it deteriorate into a full-fledged argument. So if you happen to have very strong thoughts on religion or politics, tonight might not be the right night to air them. You can be yourself without forcing your beliefs on your date, and you can be agreeable without being a pushover. Finding that balance is important because it's next to impossible to undo a first-date shouting match about the president's foreign policy in the Middle East.

Exercise simple manners. Don't start eating until both of you have your food. Talking about sex or exes can be accomplished, but only if it's clear that both of you want to go down that potentially bumpy road. Stay perpetually upbeat, no matter how you're feeling. No one wants to hear negativity (much less from a stranger). Don't bad-mouth anybody. Don't be rude to the waiter. Women should offer to pay. Men should refuse the offer. Women should thank the men.

Basic After-Date Etiquette

At the end of the date, you have to trust your instincts. If you think you have chemistry, there's nothing wrong with going for the kiss. Then again, some people don't kiss on first dates. Don't take it personally.

Tips for guys: if you think things went well, ask when you can see her again. You'll know pretty quickly if she's sincere in her response.

No matter what happens, don't push it. The last thing a woman wants is to be pressured. Be confident. Be yourself. And trust that the "right" person will appreciate that. If she doesn't? Same advice. Disregard it. She didn't deserve you anyway.

Tips for women: if you like a man, don't be afraid to give him hints during the date to let him know. We're often slow on the uptake, lacking in confidence, or just plain stupid (and sometimes all three). Eye contact, smiling, and an occasional touch on the arm are usually enough to let a man know he's got a shot.

If a date goes well, the rules shouldn't apply at all. Women may say they don't want a man to seem too eager, but if they like him, you can be sure they're glad he called the next day. I repeat: if you're a guy, and you felt there was "chemistry," you are strongly encouraged to follow up the next day, not three days later. One call can cut right through the bullshit and let a woman know you're sincere and not a player.

Conversely, if you're not having fun, or you simply aren't romantically attracted to your date (this goes for both sexes), you don't have to be an ass about it. Instead, treat your date as you'd treat a platonic friend. Maybe that's what the person was meant to be in your life, anyway. There is no value in being rude when someone else's self-esteem is on the line. I know a woman who was literally abandoned at a gas station during an Internet date. I've talked with a man whose date refused to come out of her apartment when he came to pick her up. If you don't like the way someone looks, then don't go out with him or her again. Just don't be a prick. It's not becoming.

An Exhaustive List of Dating No-nos

Here is a list of dating no-nos compiled by my friends Jennifer, Monica, and Barron. All have done their share of dating and have some very definite thoughts about things that men and women should not do when on a date.

If you're a guy, odds are you've done a bunch of these things. It's better to be aware that you're doing them than to be completely oblivious. And if you're a woman and if you're wise, you should probably look in the mirror and take your share of advice from these tips as well. It's easy to criticize the poor men who try so hard to impress you but don't know where they're going wrong; it's far more difficult to shine the light on yourself and consider the things that you do on a date that undermine your chances of being asked out again.

Tips for Men on First Dates

Do not say: "Wow, did you just wolf that chicken down?"

Do not buy her a rose in a restaurant, so she has to carry it around like a dork for the rest of the night.

Do not tell a girl that she should grow her hair any longer than it is.

Do not ask her where her hot roommate is.

Do not order a drink and then tell her she can have one if she wants.

Do not take her to an expensive restaurant and then make her feel bad for ordering too much.

Do not go to the loudest restaurant in town and then complain that you can't hear a word she is saying.

Do not pick her up with the convertible top down when it is freezing outside, just because you think it looks cool.

Do not tell her to "just relax" or "go with it" when a girl gives the signals that she wants to go home.

Do not have your assistant call to confirm your date.

Do not tell her that nothing will stop you from watching the big game.

Do not drive too fast and act like you do it all the time.

Do not openly display road rage.

Do not tell her you don't see why a girl has to buy so many clothes.

Do not go on about how this porno chick or that porno chick is so hot.

Do not mention that any other girl is hot, even if she is hot.

Do not think that if a girl agrees with you that another girl is pretty that she wants to have lesbian sex with her.

Do not look at the girl and go, "Why'd you get so dressed up?"

Do not make the girl drive.

Do not break down the bill and have her pay more because you had the pasta, but she had tuna steak.

Do not ever refer to yourself as a "wild one" or a "loose cannon" and think it sounds cool.

Do not complain about having to pay the valet parking.

Do not make her meet you somewhere and then be late, leaving her to sit at the bar alone.

Do not call on Friday at 5 P.M. to find out if she wants to go on a date that night.

Do not make her pick the restaurant.

Do not talk in a baby voice or any other voice, even if you do the greatest Austin Powers impression in the whole world.

Do not light a cigar and not ask if it will bother her.

Do not tell her that she can trust you.

Do not ever touch your date's face.

Do not brag about your abnormally large penis.

Do not wear bad shoes (women know *everything* about shoes).

Do not wear white shoes, however nice, unless you're in a seersucker suit between Memorial Day and Labor Day.

Do not wear a brown belt and black shoes, or vice versa.

Do not put cologne on your boxers.

Do not stare at your date's breasts during dinner conversation.

Do not *not* open the car door for her.

Do not tell the waiter her order without asking her first if it's okay.

Do not act too cocky or overconfident.

Tips for Women on First Dates

Do not tell him that you want to have kids in the next year.

Do not dwell on your beloved ex-boyfriend, either positively or negatively.

Do not talk about how you recently got your manic depression under control.

Do not brag about your sexual prowess.

Do not look at your watch incessantly.

Do not make a guy wait alone on your couch while you spend twenty minutes primping in the bathroom.

Do not order the most expensive bottle of wine on the menu.

Do not talk about the size of your ass or any other body part.

Do not go on and on and on about how you look. They can see.

Do not say you get drunk from one glass of wine and then proceed to drink four Manhattans.

Do not say you never kiss on the first date and then go home with him.

Do not talk about your diet and workout regimen and how much effort it is to maintain your figure. Pretend it is an accident and not a grandiose effort.

Do not eat like Ally McBeal, and if you do, don't talk about it.

Do not talk about money. It's okay to want to marry a rich old man, but keep it to yourself!

Do not complain. Save your annoyance for your friends the next day.

Do not mention it if you used to be a stripper or a prostitute.

Do not talk about clothing, makeup, or anything related to vanity and insecurity.

Do not flirt with the bartender or the waiter—unless they're female.

Do not tell him the last guy was too small.

Do not discuss any previous infections.

Do not tell him that your cat is your life.

Do not order the surf and turf unless he does as well.

Do not sit too far away.

Do not go over to his house.

Do not forget to tell him thank you and that you had a great time.

Do not tell him about another great date you recently had.

Do not show too much cleavage.

Do not offer to pay half. It's insulting.

Do not have plans afterward.

Do not let him pick you up.

Do not go to the bathroom every two minutes.

Do not tell him about your one-night stand in Mexico.

Tips for Men and Women on First Dates

Do not complain about dating.

Do not answer your cell phone while at dinner.

Do not talk about your dysfunctional family.

Do not talk about how hot your ex is, how good he/she was in bed, or how your date reminds you of him/her.

Do not go on a first date if you are sick. Reschedule.

Do not pass out under any condition (alcohol, drugs, sleep deprivation, etc.) unless you can prove you're a bonafide narcoleptic.

Do not act insecure.

Do not ogle other people at the bar.

Do not say that you feel like you have known your date forever.

Do not talk with your mouth full.

Do not bounce your leg nervously while dining.

Do not make fun of fat people, short people, or anyone with a physical condition.

Do not make racist or sexist comments.

Do not, in any subtle way, ask your date how many people he/she has slept with.

Do not wear too much perfume or cologne.

Do not be rude to the waiter.

That shouldn't be so hard, should it? Good luck and Godspeed.

"I DO NOT WANT WHAT I HAVEN'T GOT."

CHAPTER 14

Having the Serenity to Accept the Things You Cannot Change and the Courage to Change the Things You Can

Don't we all want what we can't have? Isn't that just a basic principle of life? Mariah wants a singing career like Madonna. Madonna wants an acting career like J.Lo. J.Lo wishes she could sing like Mariah.

And so on. For us noncelebs, the way this plays out are those times when a man dates a thin woman and thinks it might be fun to be with someone curvier. Or when a woman dates a cool struggling artist, but realizes that there's something pretty darned nice about being pampered by a rich doctor. Consider the fact that 35 to 40 percent of women (and 10 percent of men) dye their hair regularly. Don't we sound like a society of perpetually dissatisfied people? It shouldn't be surprising to see that this restlessness extends to our online love lives, should it?

Too Much of a Good Thing?

We should all be so lucky to have the problem of having too many choices when Internet dating. And yes, this problem sure beats the hell out of the alternative—getting no responses whatsoever. But I'm quite serious when I say that it can be a major issue if you have a constant flow of email and a limitless set of suitors from which to choose. All of these options tend to make you think that there is always something better around the corner. The result? No one is ever given a true chance, and no real intimacy is ever established. I should know. Until recently, I was a prime example of what is wrong with being "good" at Internet dating. The dating itself becomes a lifestyle instead of a means to an end, which is, ideally, finding the love of your life.

Hey, at least I recognized my flaw. I know so many serial daters who get hooked on the thrill of online dating, yet they have no clue about how much it dominates their existences. Not only do some people check their email and answering machine a dozen times a day, but there are many who simply stay online all day long at work, with their Internet dating website of choice minimized at the bottom of the screen. At this very moment, there are thousands of men and women across America who are emailing eight people at a time, talking with five on the phone, and dating three in person, but still can't help but browse online to see if there's anybody "better" out there. This can be as addicting as gambling, and with none of the financial downside, it's no surprise that the number of people dating online will have more than quadrupled from the end of 2001 to the end of 2003.

The positive news is that all the profile stuff that I discussed in this book is fixable. What can't be altered, however, is that with the online dating boom, there are too many people to divert your focus. The sheer number of members that are smiling at you in their online profiles, enticing you to write to them, even when you're totally satisfied with the person you've just started seeing, is the one thing I find hard to reconcile. This temptation to keep on looking when you already have a good thing going usually means the demise of a burgeoning relationship.

The more common problem, though, still results from members' inability to find what they're looking for. A major reason for this is that people always seem to want what they can't have. Seventy-year-old men want to date fifty-five-year-old women who want to date sixty-year-old men who want to date thirty-eight-year-old women who want to date thirty-five-year-old men who want to date twenty-seven-year-old women.

Why all this discontent and longing for the near impossible? Well, a seventy-year-old man often wants to get the youngest woman he can find. Anna Nicole Smith, anyone? Nothing wrong with wishing for that, but a fifty-five-year-old woman who still rightfully considers herself young would rather be with a peer than a guy who reminisces about the Great Depression. Problem is, the sixty-year-old men that these women covet are either going through a late midlife crisis or have never married and want children, so they end up writing to the thirty-eight-year-old women, who they think still may be within their reach. Unfortunately, for them, most thirty-eight-year-old women aren't too keen on dating men that are nearly their father's age and prefer to be with a thirty-five-year-old man who is financially stable and ready to make a commitment to having children within two years. But a lot of thirty-five-year-old guys don't really want the pressure of having to make up their minds so quickly, so they prefer dating women in their late twenties who are mature but not nearly as marriage-minded.

See why this is a problem?

Come to think of it, thirty-five-year-old men and twenty-seven-year-old women have it pretty good. But everybody else finds themselves barking up the wrong trees. Sixty-year-old women lamenting about men who want to date women younger than their daughters? Sixty-year-old men who are incredulous that despite their youthful good looks and healthy stock portfolios, the forty-year-old ladies don't seem to respond? They are sitting there, beating themselves up about something that they can't control—the wants and desires of an entire demographic. Honestly, I wish the over-fifties would just couple up to save everybody a whole lot of heartbreak. But it is not my place to police other people's wishes. The heart wants what the heart wants, although it's not always the heart that is doing the thinking for men.

Face the Facts: You're Not George Clooney

When it comes to men (and I'm focusing on men, because they, most often, are the culprits), I have no choice here but to knock some sense into their noggins, especially if they're not getting the desired results when writing to attractive women. To illustrate my point: some prime parallels from the cult of celebrity:

Julia Roberts would not have married her cameraman if he looked like Lyle Lovett. She only married Lyle Lovett because he was rich, famous, talented singer Lyle Lovett.

Christie Brinkley wouldn't have even accepted a drink from Billy Joel, except for the fact that, well, he was Billy Joel.

And until you've seen balding, bespectacled, cross-eyed author Salman Rushdie with his thirty-two-year-old model/Food Network host Padma Lakshmi, you haven't truly seen the true power of money and celebrity.

These are the exceptions to the rule. The rule is this: if you're an average guy—no multiplatinum albums, Cessna airplanes, or critically acclaimed novels to speak of—you're in for a rude awakening.

Typically, a guy approaches a hot woman, says something charming and unique that doesn't sound like it was written in *101 Cheesy Pick-up Lines*, and still finds the hot woman turning to chat with either the six-foot-three stud to her left or to the short, geeky, mega-rich Hollywood producer to her right. The sad reality is, unless you're at the far right of that looks/money bell curve, it's tough to get a shot at the supermodels of the world. But that doesn't stop every single guy on the Internet from trying.

(A brief interruption to defend myself against any claims of chauvinism, sexism, Communism, or any kind of *ism* that I haven't already considered: The paragraph above is merely a broad stereotype. I recognize this. Not all women are looking for a man with looks, power, and money, although I can't see why they wouldn't. Similarly, not every man is looking to squire around a pretty young thing with a perfect body. But stereotypes do exist for a reason. One, they are usually based on some form of truth; what's wrong with them is assuming that every individual fits that group stereotype. And two, stereotypes exist to make things simpler for writers, so we don't have to treat each individual on a case-by-case basis. This book would be way too long if I had to explain every exception to every rule. This also goes for my constant flip-flopping between "he" and "she" so as not to offend anyone's delicate sensibilities. My sincerest apologies to those who took offense at anything I wrote. Now back to our regular programming.)

Acknowledging the Competition and Looking in the Mirror

This isn't to say that every average Joe out there doesn't have a remote chance at the Cindy Crawfords of the Internet. No, not at all. You Joes should put up your pictures, write some kick-ass essays, write a personalized email that shows that you read Cindy's profile ("I just loved your performance in *Fair Game!*"), and then wait and see if you get tapped for further correspondence. Just be aware that *every other guy on the entire website is also writing to this woman.* So don't be surprised when you don't hear back from her. This may sound obvious or silly, but I've consulted with scores of "normal" (read: average-looking and not ultra-wealthy) men who have written to only the most attractive women online and are still shocked, dismayed, and even angry that they're not getting the response that they were anticipating. "They're all shallow bitches," they tell me.

Then I check out the man's profile and find that his one picture is copied from his driver's license and that his essays are all one line each: "Ask me later." Hmmm, I think Cindy has to wash her hair tonight.

This entire book has been designed to gloss up your reality and refine your personal ad—better pictures, better essays, better emails, better dating techniques—but the bottom line is this, and this is perhaps the most important thing I will say in my entire little paperback book: *You can't control what you can't control. Worry about what you can control, and let go of the rest.*

If you can honestly say that you've taken a good hard look at yourself and fixed up all of the things you can possibly fix in your profile, your job is done. Congratulations. Whatever happens now is out of your hands. This is not intended as a sarcastic consolation prize as much as it is a vital reminder: if someone doesn't appreciate your profile, then they're simply not the right person for you. Forget 'em and move on.

If someone doesn't write back to you, there's no point in worrying. You can't bludgeon someone into liking you, no matter how much it would seem from your profiles that you two are undeniably compatible.

I've talked to a bunch of people who have signed up for services just to meet one person and when that person didn't respond, they just gave up on online dating entirely. It sounds irrational, but one of the first things I said in here is that people have a tendency to throw common sense out the window when it comes to dating. And guess what? It's very easy to build up a fantasy about someone based on a few pictures and an eloquent essay that personally speaks to you. I've done it myself.

The trouble arises when you put all your eggs in one basket and convince yourself that you and a total stranger are soul mates. That's when you find yourself writing some freaky love letter like that nice guy who sees his mom for dinner three times a week. Please don't fall into that trap. There are a lot of other fish in the sea, and they're just waiting to get caught. That's why they signed up. Don't think for one second that it's the end of the world just because someone you're excited about isn't all that excited about you. I'm not one to believe in things being "meant to be," but if someone doesn't write back to you, clearly that is a relationship that is not "meant to be."

The Magic Formula You've All Been Waiting For

I'm always telling people that online dating takes three things: creativity, patience, and resilience. The creativity will help you construct your winning profile and your witty emails; the patience is necessary, because if you go into this thinking that you're going to fall in love in a month, you're bound to be disappointed; and resilience is a must, because in a forum like this, with millions of single people optimistically hoping to find "the one," most of us are going to have to first meet a lot of people who are not "the one." That means there's going to be rejection. Lots of it. And if your self-esteem isn't in good shape, then this may be a rough medium for you.

Unfortunately, no book can imbue you with self-esteem if you don't have it already. This guide is solely intended to prepare you adequately for what to expect in the sea of Internet dating and how to navigate its choppy waters. It can't prepare you for real-life experience any more than a pre-med class can prepare a doctor for performing surgery. But, like a class, if you absorb the information and keep it in the back of your mind (or at the front of your bookshelf), it may just save your ass when it's time for the big test.

"HONESTY ...
IS SUCH A
LONELY WORD."

Why Being Yourself Is the Only Way to Successfully Find Love Online

Before publishing this book, I showed it to over a dozen trusted friends to get their feedback. Nobody ever doubted the message that I was trying to convey but, rather, the way in which it was conveyed. But the language in this how-to guide was not an accident or an over-sight. It's intentionally irreverent, blunt, silly, and, hopefully, helpful. Most of all, it's honest. I made a point to write not what people wanted to hear but rather what people needed to hear.

It's the difference between talking with a trusted friend as opposed to an acquaintance. The trusted friend may take you aside one day and tell you that you've been acting like a real jerk recently and want to know what's up, while the acquaintance will most likely write you off as a real jerk and never even tell you that she has given up on you. I'm trying to be the trusted friend here.

The truth hurts. However, if you don't have the truth, you're liv-ing in your own fantasyland, which is a world that nobody occupies but you. That's lonely. It has to be extremely difficult to make informed dating decisions if you're not seeing things like the rest of the world sees them. You may think you have good pictures up, you may think you have strong essays, you may think that you have a good system for writing other members, you may think that your singledom is everybody else's fault. But if you're not getting results, the only place to look is within.

Insecurity: The Silent Killer

If people are reading your profile and it's not an accurate portrayal of you, the only person you're hurting is yourself. From the second you go on that first date, you are a fraud who is going to be exposed sooner or later. If you act comfortable in your skin from the very outset of the relationship, you'll be amazed at how many people will appreciate you for it. And why? Because so many people are *not* themselves when they go out. They try to be what they think the other person wants, which is an act that has a rather short half-life.

Honesty and self-confidence are probably the most important assets you can have as an online dater. If you come to the table with both of those, you'll be unstoppable, because you'll be all you. Isn't that what everyone wants out of a relationship? To be themselves, to be loved and not judged for it?

I'm the first to concede that Internet dating can be huge and overwhelming and even scary to some. But it's not going away. You can fight the trend all you like, but I think you're better off mastering the medium than pretending it doesn't exist. Otherwise you get left behind, stubborn, sad, and single. And those are just the S's.

A Final Contradiction from Yours Truly

Although I stressed the concept that you shouldn't consider online dating to be a numbers game, when you get right down to it, it is. You do have to meet a whole bunch of people in order to find the one person who's perfect for you. Online dating is just the forum that allows you to meet those people. After you make contact, you're on your own.

All my warnings and finger-wagging and no-nos are solely designed to prevent you from making the same mistakes that I did during my arduous journey to become an online dating consultant.

Please understand that online dating is not just my job but also a huge part of my life. I couldn't imagine dating these past four years without the Internet, and I hope I've been able to pass on some of my enthusiasm to you.

We all know that there are no guarantees in dating. Anyone who suggests otherwise isn't telling you the truth. But if you follow some of the advice offered in this book, you stand an excellent chance of meeting some good people. That's your only job. Meet them. Who knows? Maybe one will even be the one who makes you want to quit online dating and start shopping for a catering hall and a band.

The basics, we've covered: detailed, thoughtful, heartfelt, positive, funny, spell-checked essays are good. Recent, smiling, active pictures that show you with friends, family, and favorite hobbies are good. Concise, personalized emails that respond to something specific in someone's profile are good. Wit, class, curiosity, and positivity are good, whether you're talking about essays, emails, or dates.

This is all common sense.

What seems to evade most people is that, at the end of the day, your most important asset is your honesty. If you're not honest with yourself about who you are and what you're looking for, you're wasting your time, as well as the time of a very nice person on the other end. But if you're true to yourself—and you're true to others—you're well on your way to finding that special someone.

You just gotta give it some time.

The End